The Well-Dressed Puppet

Bound to Create

You are a creator.

Whatever your form of expression — photography, filmmaking, animation, games, audio, media communication, web design, or theatre — you simply want to create without limitation. Bound by nothing except your own creativity and determination.

Focal Press can help.

For over 75 years Focal has published books that support your creative goals. Our founder, Andor Kraszna-Krausz, established Focal in 1938 so you could have access to leading-edge expert knowledge, techniques, and tools that allow you to create without constraint. We strive to create exceptional, engaging, and practical content that helps you master your passion.

Focal Press and you.

Bound to create.

> We'd love to hear how we've helped you create. Share your experience:
> **www.focalpress.com/boundtocreate**

Focal Press
Taylor & Francis Group

The Well-Dressed Puppet

A Guide to Creating Puppet Costumes

Cheralyn Lambeth

NEW YORK AND LONDON

First published 2015
by Focal Press
70 Blanchard Road, Suite 402, Burlington, MA 01803

and by Focal Press
2 Park Square, Milton Park, Abingdon, Oxon OX14 4RN

Focal Press is an imprint of the Taylor & Francis Group, an informa business

© 2015 Taylor & Francis

The right of Cheralyn Lambeth to be identified as author of this work has been asserted by her in accordance with sections 77 and 78 of the Copyright, Designs and Patents Act 1988.

All rights reserved. No part of this book may be reprinted or reproduced or utilised in any form or by any electronic, mechanical, or other means, now known or hereafter invented, including photocopying and recording, or in any information storage or retrieval system, without permission in writing from the publishers.

Notices
Knowledge and best practice in this field are constantly changing. As new research and experience broaden our understanding, changes in research methods, professional practices, or medical treatment may become necessary.

Practitioners and researchers must always rely on their own experience and knowledge in evaluating and using any information, methods, compounds, or experiments described herein. In using such information or methods they should be mindful of their own safety and the safety of others, including parties for whom they have a professional responsibility.

Product or corporate names may be trademarks or registered trademarks, and are used only for identification and explanation without intent to infringe.

Library of Congress Cataloging in Publication Data
Lambeth, Cheralyn.
    The well-dressed puppet: a guide to creating puppet costumes/ Cheralyn Lambeth.
      pages cm
    Includes bibliographical references and index.
    ISBN 978-1-138-02533-2 (pbk.)
    1. Puppet making. 2. Doll clothes. 3. Costume. I. Title.
    TT174.7.L36 2015
    745.592'24—dc23   2014007465

ISBN: 978-1-138-02533-2 (pbk)
ISBN: 978-1-315-77516-6 (ebk)

Typeset in FS Albert
By Keystroke, Station Road, Codsall, Wolverhampton

Printed and bound in India by Replika Press Pvt. Ltd.

Contents

Acknowledgement ix
Introduction xi

1 How to get started — 1

But first… a basic glossary of puppet types and puppet theatre terms — 1
List of supplies—tools, building materials, and other helpful items — 6
As you think about creating your puppet's costume — 9
Types of fabrics you might want to use — 10
Basic sewing techniques and helpful hints — 13

2 Types of costumes (or how to costume for your type of puppet) — 19

Permanent costumes vs removable — 20
Using store-bought clothing — 22
Things to consider when costuming… — 25
   …Marionettes — 25
   …Hand/rod puppets (and puppets with practical hands) — 28
   …Hand puppets with legs — 30

3	**Creating costumes for non-human puppets**	**33**
	Costuming odd-shaped puppets (and/or those without arms and legs)	33
	Costuming puppets with multiple limbs	39
4	**How to create and construct basic patterns**	**49**
	How to use the patterns in this book (and how to do the photocopier trick)	49
	Constructing the patterns	53
5	**Accessories**	**63**
	Wigs/hairpieces	63
	Hair construction techniques	67
	Glasses	69
	Jewelry	70
	Gloves	71
	Ties (and other neck adornments)	71
	Shoes	73
	Hats and other headwear	75
6	**Props**	**83**
	Ladies' hand fan	87
	Drawstring bag	90
	Broom (and Tiny Tim's crutch)	97
	Books	98
7	**Some costume ideas to help you get started**	**105**
	Fairy-tale princess	105
	Fairy-tale prince (or pirate)	109
	Witch	116
	Wizard	117

	Little Red Riding Hood	123
	Angel	127
8	**The patterns**	**133**
	Basic shirt/bodice front	134
	Basic shirt/bodice back	135
	Robe	136
	Robe Extension	137
	Basque bodice front	138
	Fitted sleeve	139
	Gathered sleeve	140
	Robe sleeve	141
	Pants	142
	Tie	143
	Basic hat	144
	Pointed hat	145
	Crown	146
	Basic shoe	147
	Cape with hood	148
	Pointed hood	149
	Angel wing	150
	Beard	151
	Basic hand puppet body	152
	Resources	153
	Bibliography	157
	Author biography	159
	Index	161

Acknowledgment

For their help with their project, I owe a huge debt of gratitude to Drew Allison at Grey Seal Puppets (www.greysealpuppets.com), who freely gave advice and constructive criticism when needed, as well as allowing me to use many of Grey Seal's amazing puppets in photos throughout the book. I also want to thank my fellow puppeteer, Vania Reckard, for her technical advice, both during writing and editing; Megan Guidry for her technical assistance with the patterns; Rhonda Hedger for sharing the "photocopier trick"; and fellow costumers Jeffrey Hawley, Cricket Bauer, and M. Doc Geressy for their advice with many of the sewing/costuming items. This book has been a long time in the making, and I couldn't have done it without you all!

Introduction

So… you're producing a puppet show! You've written the script, touched up your stage, and built a cast of characters. What more could you need? On with the show!

But wait—there's much more to a puppet production than just the puppet. Although you can create an effective show with only a bare stage and, a simple puppet, the technical elements of a theatrical production—sets, props, and in particular, costumes—can add a great deal to your performance and help create the mood for your show. Your puppet is a performer with a role to play, and—just as with human actors—the costume is a large part of defining that role.

Costuming and costume accessories can greatly expand the ability of your puppet to perform a wide variety of roles. They can also add believability to your puppet's character as well as help establish the geographical and historical setting of your play (for instance, a little girl dressed in a red hooded cloak and carrying a basket can be none other than Little Red Riding Hood on her way to Grandmother's house). Your puppet's costume can show your audience, at a single glance, information about your play that you might otherwise have to verbally explain in your script.

Throughout this book, there are basic costume patterns and construction techniques that should be helpful to the beginner as well as the more advanced puppet costumer. I've also included boxes featuring Tricks of the Trade that

Trick of the Trade

You'll see these boxes throughout the book.

other costumers use in their work. Finally, in addition to basic costume construction, there is information on how to put together accessories—shoes, hats, etc.—to complement your puppet's wardrobe and add to their character.

Now, at this point you may well be thinking, "That all sounds extremely complicated. Why can't I just go out and buy doll or children's clothes, and alter those to fit my puppet?" You certainly can do that in many cases, and in fact that topic is discussed in a chapter further on. But just in case your local department store doesn't carry a miniature eighteenth-century gown for your puppet production of *The Magic Flute*, you'll want to know how to make your own. And that's what this book is all about!

Meet Herbert. You'll see him throughout the book in various roles—hand puppet, marionette glove puppet, etc.—helping to demonstrate the different types

Figure I.1 Meet Herbert, your friendly puppet costume guide

Introduction

of costuming needed for different types of puppets. He'll be your guide as you work on your own costumes—from choosing fabrics, to making a pattern, to building the costume, and finally, to adding hairstyles and accessories for the perfect finishing touch. With Herbert's help and your own imagination, you'll be able to give your production a style that's all your own.

Now, on with the show!

chapter 1

How to get started

But first... a basic glossary of puppet types and puppet theatre terms

Before you can begin to costume your puppet, it will be helpful to know just what type of puppet(s) you are working with, as this can affect the techniques and materials you'll use. Different types of puppets have different elements to consider when building their costumes and props, and these will play a part in determining how you costume around them. In addition, these terms (along with some basic theatre terms) will be referenced throughout the book; we'll start with a list of these terms so that, when you see them later in the book, you'll know exactly what's being discussed!

Let's start with a list of the common types of puppets and the elements that control them.

Hand puppet: As the name implies, this is a type of puppet that fits over the puppeteer's hand/arm, and is moved by the fingers and hand of the wearer. (One type of simple hand puppet is also known as a glove puppet, which generally has a soft, hollow body that fits over the puppeteer's hand like a glove and is manipulated by

Figure 1.1 Herbert as a simple hand/glove puppet. Here the puppet's body fits over the puppeteer's hand like a glove

the performer's fingers). These puppets generally do not have legs or a lower body which will be seen; a puppet sleeve gives the illusion of the rest of the puppet's body and covers the puppeteer's arm. With the exception of marionettes (discussed further on), most puppets fall in this category, and may have additional features such as a moving mouth and hand rods.

Moving mouth puppet: This is a type of hand puppet in which the mouth is articulated, most often by the puppeteer's hand/fingers. It is quite often built of flexible materials (foam and/or fabric) which allow the puppeteer's thumb to operate the lower jaw while the remaining fingers control the upper jaw. The puppeteer can then open and close the mouth of the puppet as it speaks.

Figure 1.2 A simple moving mouth turtle puppet

Rod puppet: There are two different types of rod puppets. One type consists of a single figure (which may have simple articulated parts or be a solid piece) that is built around a central wooden or metal rod used to support and control the body, and which is held and manipulated by the puppeteer. The other is known as a hand-and-rod puppet, in which the mouth is operated by the puppeteer's hand as defined above, while the puppet's arms are controlled by rods. These can be controlled either by a single puppeteer who operates the mouth with one hand and the rods with the other, or by two or more puppeteers, allowing for a much greater range of motion.

1 How to Get Started

Practical hand puppet: In this type of puppet, one of the puppeteer's hands becomes a hand of the puppet itself. As with the hand-and-rod puppet, the performer operates the head with one hand and the puppet's hand with the other; in some cases, another puppeteer will operate the other hand. (Additional information on practical hand puppets, and how to costume around them, is discussed in the next chapter.)

Marionette: A puppet operated from above by strings attached to its head and limbs.

Figure 1.3 A simple central-rod puppet, carved of wood, with loose-hanging arms that move freely as the puppet is manipulated. This type of historical puppet is known as a Wayang Golek, a classical character from Indonesian puppet theatre. *(Wayang Golek appears courtesy of Grey Seal Puppets)*

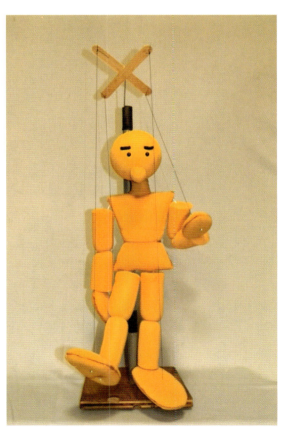

Figure 1.4 Herbert as a marionette

Figure 1.5 A smaller version of Herbert as a simple finger puppet. Here, any needed costuming can be created as part of his body, as opposed to having a piece for a body and building a separate costume to dress it with

Trick of the Trade

Most puppeteers find it useful to sew rings to the bottom hem of their puppets, and install corresponding cup hooks along the inside of their puppet stage on which to hang the puppets for easy access during the performance.

Figure 1.6 A ring sewn to the bottom edge of the puppet sleeve, used to hang the puppet from a hook set on the inside of the stage for easy access during the puppet performance

Shadow puppet: A shadow puppet is a simple, flat articulated figure attached to thin rods or wires and operated between a light source and a screen to cast shadows, giving the impression of moving people or other three-dimensional objects. While most of the time the puppet itself is a flat piece that is never seen, and so doesn't require an actual costume, it may need detailing to give it the illusion of costuming, particularly if it's a recreation of an existing puppet.

Finger puppet: As the name implies, this type of puppet is used on only one of the puppeteer's fingers, and by its very nature is generally small and simple. Building elaborate costumes for these types of puppet is impractical, and most often the body and costume can be created as one piece.

Now that we have a general idea of the types of puppets we'll be working with, let's take a look at some of the basic theatre terms you'll also see throughout the book.

Stage: The performance area, often raised above the audience, on which the puppets perform. Generally, the puppeteer is hidden behind the stage set up, which is topped by a play board.

Play board: The area running along the top of the puppet stage, and the main performance area. This can be made of a flat board, a piece of fabric, or other type of material.

Backdrop: A cloth or other flat material behind the back of the stage to create a background for the performance. It can be painted as scenery, or be a simple black fabric for a more neutral background.

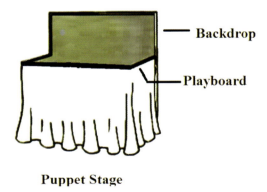

Figure 1.7 Diagram of puppet theatre set-up

While these terms may not be essential to creating costumes for your puppets, they are an integral part of puppet theatre, and can be useful as you progress in knowledge and understanding of puppetry. Having covered some of the basics related to your puppets, let's now start to build costumes for them!

A list of useful supplies and basic sewing techniques

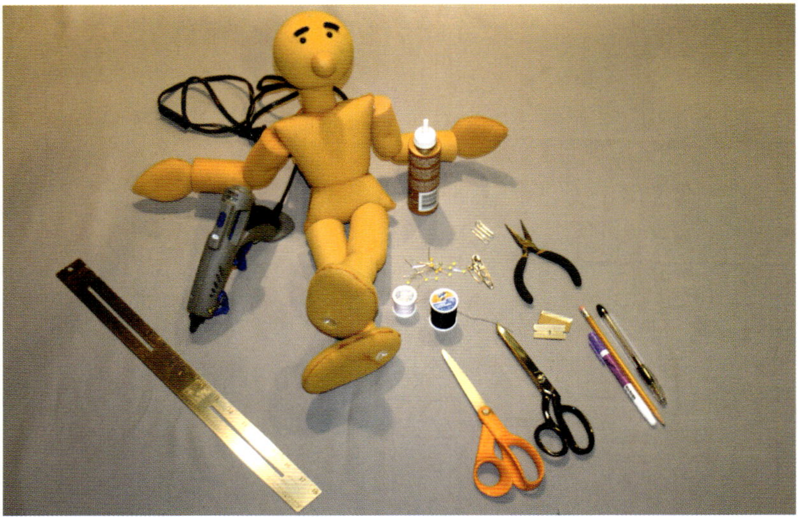

Figure 1.8 Some of the supplies you'll need for your costume creations

This next section contains a list of materials you'll need to begin creating your own costumes, as well as simple sewing instructions. I've tried to come up with as complete a supply list as possible, and found it got *very* long after a while! You may not need or use every one of these items, but I have found all of them to come in handy at one point or another during the building process. The materials which are most essential have stars by them.

*Sewing machine: For the purpose of creating puppet costumes, a simple straight and zigzag stitch machine will work perfectly well. These can be found very inexpensively at department stores, and include brands such as Singer and Brother. It is also helpful to make sure that the throat plate—the metal plate underneath the needle on your machine—has ruled markings for showing you where to line up the edge of your fabric when stitching, to give you a measured seam allowance.

Serger: Not totally necessary, and in fact it can be extremely difficult to serge all the tiny seams in your puppet's garments. But it's a quick and easy way to construct a long straight seam, and can create a fast finished edge on a garment hem.

Figure 1.9 An older model Kenmore sewing machine, still in good working condition, and very good for general home sewing

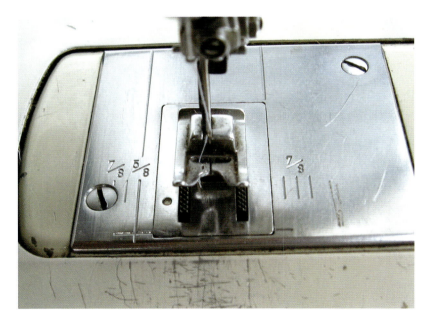

Figure 1.10 Be sure to choose a machine that has a marked throat plate. If you find a machine you like that does not have a marked throat plate, you can generally purchase a replacement that does from your machine's manufacturer

Trick of the Trade

You can create your own curved needle from a straight sewing needle. Holding the eye end of the needle with a pair of pliers, run the needle through a candle flame until it becomes almost red-hot. Then, using another pair of pliers, *carefully* bend the hot needle into a gentle curve (don't bend too much, or your needle will break). Be sure to wear gloves for safety, and wipe away any soot before you sew with your needle.

*Hand sewing needles of various sizes: Also, curved needles, such as those available for quilting, are *great* for this kind of work. You can generally find those along with regular needles at your local fabric store. Or, if you happen to have a friend in the medical or veterinary professions, you might be able to have them find curved surgical needles for you.

*Thread: Different types—regular machine thread, hand sewing thread (such as upholstery, quilter's, or buttonhole twist), embroidery floss in different colors, "invisible" nylon thread. Metallic threads can be used to create interesting decoration, but these tend to fray and can be difficult to sew with. You might also want to purchase beeswax to coat your thread for hand sewing—this will smooth out the thread and make it easier to sew with.

Glues: *White craft glue, *hot glue gun and sticks, tacky glue, rubber cement. Also in this category—products like Fray-Check or Stop-Fray, which are solutions used to prevent the raw edges of fabric from raveling. These can also be found at your local fabric store.

*Cutting tools: Scissors (one pair *just for fabrics*, and a separate pair for paper and other non-fabric materials). Razor blades, X-acto knives. Also, a pair of heavy-duty industrial shears (such as those available from the Gingher scissor company) can come in handy. A small rotary cutter with blades, embroidery scissors (great for those tiny seams) and seam rippers will also prove very useful. You may want to invest in a cutting mat as well.

*Ruler, yardstick, measuring tape

Needle nose pliers, regular pliers, wire cutters, hole punch

Wire: Milliner's wire (a flexible, fabric-wrapped wire used by hat makers), floral wire.

Various papers and paper board: Craft paper and tracing paper for patterns, cardboard, poster board, foam core, construction paper (especially metallics).

*Iron, ironing board, and sleeve board: You can also create a puppet-size sleeve board by stitching a tube of fabric, stuffing it tightly with Polyfill or cotton batting (also useful materials to have!), and stitching both ends closed.

Rigilene, plastic tubing (you can get plastic polyethylene tubing in different weights and diameters at hardware/home improvement stores—we call it pod tubing, although in real life it's actually used for plumbing), **dress boning.**

Interfacing (various weights): I prefer the fusible (iron-on) kind as opposed to the sew-in kind. Another useful sewing material is Stitch-Witchery (also known as Wonder-Under)—these are fusible webs that heat-bond fabrics together using an iron, and can be used to create fast, non-sew hems.

*Safety pins and straight pins

Paper clips: These are good for holding together fabric that might show pin holes as you sew. Be sure to remove the paper clips from your fabric before you sew over them!

Clothes pins: Good for holding glued items together as they dry.

Fabric-paper paints and brushes of various sizes: Such as acrylic and specialty fabric paint. "Puffy" paint is especially good for creating textures.

Pens, pencils, markers: Chalk and disappearing markers are also good to have.

And finally, **fabrics and trims:** Yarn, ribbon, leather scraps, beads, felt, buttons, jewelry findings, etc. I'll talk more about what types of fabrics and trims are best to use later on.

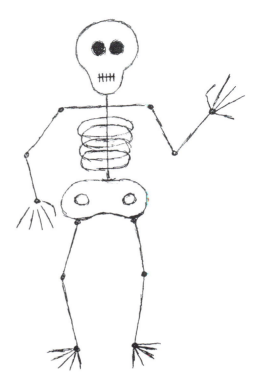

Figure 1.12 Not *this* kind of boning

As you think about creating your puppet's costume

When designing a costume and choosing fabrics, think about your puppet's character and what your puppet will be required to do during the performance. Remember that your puppet is not necessarily the same thing as a doll, which may have a complete costume that can be taken off and changed. Also unlike a doll, your puppet will be moved about in performance, and will very likely have all sorts of strings, rods, hand openings, etc. that you'll need to worry about costuming around. Not only will the costume need to define your puppet's character, it will also need to be light enough for you to hold comfortably for the duration of your performance and to move with the puppet, and designed to accommodate the strings, rods, and hand openings.

As you begin to create your costume, there are shortcuts you can take to avoid adding unnecessary weight and stiffness to your puppet. Unless your puppet needs to change costume pieces during its performance, or have a variety of roles to play during its lifetime, there is often no need to make a complete costume that can be changed. Pockets don't need to be real; a shirt front "bib," sewn to the puppet itself and hidden beneath a coat or jacket, can be used instead of an entire shirt; and you can use paint instead of actual trims/braids/buttons. Not only will this make your costume lighter, it will also cut down on construction costs and time.

Even though you may be using these construction shortcuts, you'll still want your costume to last, and good workmanship is important. So make your costume sturdy! One important thing you can do is choose a good-quality, long-wearing fabric as the base of your costume, especially if your puppet will see a lot of stage action. (There is a list of suggested fabrics further on.) It may mean using a more expensive fabric to get the look you want. As your puppet is likely fairly small, though, you can use very small scraps of fabric to build your puppet's clothing, and can create a rich and elaborate-looking costume with a minimum of expense. The investment will certainly be worth it!

Types of fabrics you might want to use

When you begin looking for costume fabrics, be sure to pay close attention to the "drape" of the fabric—how well it hangs from all directions—and to the pattern/textures on both the front and the back. Quite often, the "wrong" side of the fabric can be more interesting than the "right" side! You'll also want to avoid very thick and stiff fabrics such as heavy velvets and upholstery fabrics. Not only are they extremely difficult to sew on a small scale, they will also hang stiffly on your puppet and can restrict movement. Fabrics that are *too* thin, though, can allow light to shine through, so medium-weight materials are usually the best. Also, bear in mind that large print fabrics may not show up as well on a small puppet as they would on a larger costume; so be sure that any prints you choose are in keeping with the scale of your puppet. You might even need to paint or stencil your own pattern onto fabric to get the look you want.

Here's Herbert wearing an outfit with a large print…

1 How to Get Started

Figure 1.13 Herbert in a large print fabric…

Figure 1.14 …and in a smaller print, which is much more effective

…and a fabric with a smaller print design. Depending on the look you want to achieve, the smaller-scale pattern will read much better on the smaller size of your puppet.

Lastly, bear in mind that it is the overall line, silhouette, and colors of your costume that truly matter, as opposed to intricate patterns and details. Your audience will likely be seated some distance from the stage and your puppets, and so will probably not notice tiny particulars on the costumes. In theatre, there's a general guideline called the "30-foot rule"; costumes, set pieces, and props simply need to look as you would want them to look from 30 feet away.

Figure 1.15 The character Rumplestiltskin in a prison uniform. Here the black stripes have been painted onto the base fabric to achieve the desired scale and effect. *(Rumplestiltskin appears courtesy of Grey Seal Puppets)*

Here are some suggested materials to keep in mind when making your puppet costumes:

- light velvets (stretch velvets are particularly good)
- medium-weight cottons
- polyester knits
- chiffons and gauzes (remember, however, that these types of fabric tend to fray and ravel easily)
- small prints
- metallics (these are great for creating an exotic look for your costumes. As with chiffons and gauzes, though, they tend to fray and ravel easily, and also—very important!—*will melt* if you iron them on too high a setting!)
- fabrics cut from old clothes or curtains found at thrift stores. These will not be as stiff as brand new fabric, and will already have a "lived-in" look.

Choose fabrics that will complement your puppet and won't clash with any background scenery you might have. You'll also want to see the effect your stage lighting will have on the fabrics and paints you are considering for your puppet's costume. Try to look at your colors and materials under the lighting conditions you plan to use for your performance, to be certain that you will achieve the desired effect.

Note: In television puppetry, however, details *are* extremely important, as the camera will pick up and magnify any problems in your puppet or its costume. Make certain you don't have any flaws (such as loose threads, smeared paint, etc.), and pay careful attention to construction details. Some colors and prints will not work as well on the television screen as others. Be aware that all black and too much of other dark colors can absorb light; fabrics with changeable weaves and busy prints can create confusing patterns on the screen; shiny fabrics (such as metallics and satins) can cause unwanted reflections; and white should be used sparingly as it can create a glare and throw off the color balance of the overall picture. If possible, use cream or off-white instead—it will still read as white on the screen.

Trick of the Trade

If you are doing any work involving chroma-key in a TV production, be certain you do *not* use the key color (generally green or blue) in any part of your puppet or its costume. Otherwise, that part of your puppet will disappear into the background in the final edit!

In addition to choosing sturdy, durable fabrics to give your puppet's costume a long and useful life, you'll want to be sure your construction techniques are strong as well. Knot off your hand sewing thread; backstitch on all your machine seams (if you're not entirely certain what is meant by this term, don't worry, there's an explanation of that and other sewing terms further on); secure any fabric or seams that are raveling with a product like Fray-Check or Stop-Fray; and use a good craft glue or bridal cement to secure any trims, beads, etc. It is generally a good idea to sew trims and beads whenever possible instead of gluing them; glue can stiffen the fabric, which would be especially noticeable on the smaller scale of your puppet's costume. It also makes it harder to remove the bead or trim later on if you should change your mind.

Basic sewing techniques and helpful hints

You don't need to be an expert stitcher to create a costume for your puppet. However, some knowledge of sewing is useful when constructing a costume, and is a good thing to have in any case! If you have little or no sewing experience, it might be worth your while to check into a basic sewing book (I highly recommend *The Reader's Digest Guide Complete Guide to Sewing*; even

Figure 1.16 A hand-sewn running stitch

Figure 1.17 A hand-sewn back stitch

advanced/professional stitchers often refer to this book!). Here is a list of many of the basic sewing terms you'll see throughout this book, and that you'll use as you construct your costume:

Straight or running stitch: On your machine, this is the standard sewing stitch; by hand, this stitch can be created by running your needle in and out of the fabric.

Back stitch: On your machine, this is the reverse stitch you'll generally use to lock off the start and end of a straight stitch (seam) to keep it from pulling loose. By hand, a backstitch is created by sewing stitches backwards to the direction of sewing. This not only locks off your thread and keeps it from pulling out, but it can also be used to create stitching lines to outline shapes and add detail for embroidery. To create a backstitch, first thread your needle and knot your thread, then run your needle down and back up through the fabric to form your first stitch running along the underside of your fabric. Pull the thread back towards your knot and run the needle into the same spot as your knot; pull taut so that the thread lies smooth against the fabric. Run the needle up through your fabric to create your second underside stitch, pull the thread through, then run the needle back into the end of your first stitch to form your second stitch line; pull thread taut. Repeat the process until your line of stitches reaches your desired length.

Basting Stitch: A basting stitch is a large hand or machine stitch used to hold your fabric in place securely before you sew it together, and then removed afterwards. You can baste fabric together by using the longest stitch setting on your machine, or by sewing a running stitch by hand with long stitches. I've found it very helpful to hand-baste pieces together before I machine stitch them if they are particularly tiny or if the fabric is very slippery (such as satin).

Gathering Stitch: This type of stitch is often used to gather a larger piece of fabric into a smaller one, such as the edge of sleeve into an armhole, or the top of skirt into a waistband. It can be created in several ways. If your garment is really small, it is often easier to hand-sew a large running stitch across the edge to be gathered (do *not* knot off your thread just yet), then pull your thread to ruffle the fabric. Or, you can do a gathering stitch on your machine by using the longest stitch setting and sewing *two* rows of straight stitches along your seam line approximately $\frac{1}{8}$" apart; pull the bobbin (bottom) thread to gather the fabric.

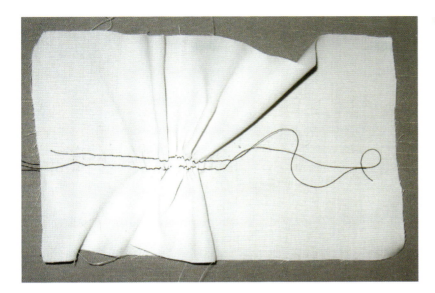

Figure 1.18 Machine gathering stitch

Another method of creating a gathering stitch on your machine is by using a small zigzag stitch and a length of heavy thread (such as upholstery thread or buttonhole twist). Lay the upholstery thread across your seam line, then zigzag over it (being careful to not catch the length of thread in your stitch). Pull the upholstery thread at each end to gather your fabric.

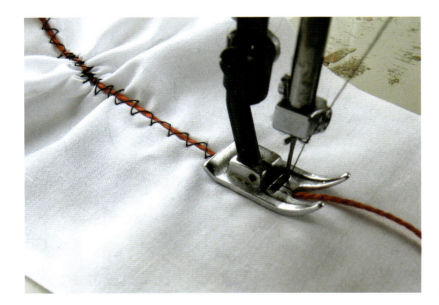

Figure 1.19 Using the zigzag stitch on your machine to create a gathering stitch

Figure 1.20 A simple turned hem

Trick of the Trade

You can create a fast decorative hem by serging it using a thread in your serger that contrasts with your fabric.

Figure 1.21 Creating a dart in a garment

Hem: A hem is the finish for the bottom edge of a garment. For puppet costumes, a turned-up hem, or "shirt-tail hem"—taking the raw edge of the garment, turning it a small width twice towards the wrong side of the fabric, and machine-stitching it down—is probably the only type of hem you'll need. You can also secure the hem by hand after you've turned the edge up if you don't want a stitch line to show. If you have hand puppets whose lower garment edge will never show above the stage, there is often no need to completely finish off a hem; however, *some* type of finished edge, such as serging or zigzagging, should be done to keep your fabric from fraying. In many cases, especially in hand puppets, the hem of the costume serves as the puppet sleeve hiding the puppeteer's arm; while these may not need a traditional hem, you don't want to cut the sleeve off abruptly and ruin the illusion of the puppet's pants or skirt below the stage play board.

Dart: A dart is used to help shape a garment for a more fitted look. Darts are created by stitching a wedge-shaped fold of fabric to taper the fabric and fit it snugly against the wearer.

Drape/draping: This is a pattern-making technique in which you place fabric (generally not your "real" fabric, but a test fabric of similar weight to the one your costume will be made of) directly on to your puppet to create a pattern. Once you have the fabric secured to your puppet, you can then make any markings on it to transfer the shape of the puppet, as well as the placement of darts, seams, arm/leg openings, etc. Draping is especially useful for puppets with an odd shape and/or multiple arms and legs.

"Face" of the fabric: The "front" or "right" side of the fabric.

Facing: A fabric used to finish the raw edges of a garment, such as at the armholes and/or neckline.

Mock-up: A "first draft" of your costume. Once you have created a pattern for your puppet's costume, either from a flat pattern or by draping it, you can construct a mock-up of test fabric and fit it to your puppet to make any needed adjustments.

Seam allowance: The seam allowance is the amount of extra fabric added to the stitching line of your pattern, and can range from ¼" wide to several inches. Most commercial patterns for home sewing have ⅝" added; while the patterns in this book do not have seam allowance already added (to allow for scaling the patterns up/down), I generally recommend adding a seam allowance of ¼" for smaller patterns.

Selvage: Selvage is the finished edge running along each side of a piece of uncut fabric. Quite often, a selvage edge can be used in place of a sewn finished hem or other edge.

Serging: Serging is the binding-off of an edge of fabric, to prevent it from unravelling/fraying. It can be done with a serger (a machine specifically for that purpose) or by running a tight zig-zag stitch down the edge of your fabric.

With these basic sewing terms and procedures in mind, you can start to plan out your puppet's costume! These techniques will become familiar to you once you've completed a garment or two, and you won't even need to refer back to the instructions.

chapter 2

Types of costumes

(or how to costume for your type of puppet)

Before you start to plan out a costume, look at your puppet and determine its characteristics, as well as what will be required of it and its costume. You'll find that different types of costuming and construction techniques will be needed for different types of puppets. How much will your puppet be required to move? Will any part of its costume actually need to be functional? How much of a costume do you really need? These factors, along with the type of puppet you have—hand/rod, marionette—will all determine what goes into making your puppet's costume.

While generally all puppets will need to move during the course of a performance—movement is, after all, what puppetry is about—some may have more movement than others. A simple rod puppet without any type of articulation or a puppet without arms or legs may be able to sustain a closer fitting, glued-on costume much better than one that has moveable limbs. In addition, you may generally not need a functional pocket, or buttons/fasteners that actually work, on your puppet's costume, unless your story calls for the character to pull something out of its pocket or change its costume; in cases such as these, then, you'll want to make certain that those features are incorporated into the costume. Lastly, it's most often the overall line and silhouette, not the intricate details, which are most important for conveying the idea of your puppet's costume. You can quite often get by with only the suggestion of certain clothing items—such as a shirt front under a coat, or painted trim—as opposed to creating a complete costume.

Permanent costumes vs removable

While many puppets are "people-shaped," not every puppet is equipped with the standard one head/two arms/two legs. Some may have four or more arms; some may have no arms at all. Still others may have additional appendages such as wings or a tail, while some puppets may be fashioned after a completely inanimate object. In this case especially it's often much easier to construct your puppet's costume permanently on to its body.

As mentioned in the previous chapter, there is often no need to make a complete costume that can be changed. If your puppet is only going to be used in one performance, or will play the same character throughout the course of its lifetime, you can create a permanent or semi-permanent costume for it. The main advantage of a costume that is permanently attached to your puppet's body is that it's generally easier to construct. One of the great things about building a costume for puppets (as opposed to building costumes for people) is that you can create an entire outfit by simply placing the fabric directly onto your puppet's body, trimming it to fit, and stitching or gluing it into place. (This can work equally well even on people-shaped puppets. Just make certain to allow yourself enough fabric in the costume for your puppet to move freely, and be careful when gluing—stiff glue seams can restrict movement).

In many cases, the puppet's body and costume are constructed in one piece, as in a simple hand puppet. Details such as coat lapels, buttons, etc. can be stitched or glued on after the body is assembled. As with all costumes, make sure your fabric and seams are sturdy enough to handle the stress of performing, and will last your puppet's lifetime.

Even if your puppet has a costume change during a single performance, you can achieve that by constructing two or more of the same puppet in its various costumes. It will mean extra work at the beginning of

Figure 2.1 Herbert as a simple hand puppet. In this case the costume and body are constructed as one piece. Costume changes, if needed, can be accomplished by putting your puppet's head on a different body

2 Types of costumes

Figure 2.2 The character Humpty Dumpty. His elaborate costume, along with his arms and legs, are permanently glued to the plastic egg shape that makes up his body. *(Humpty Dumpty appears courtesy of Grey Seal Puppets)*

Figure 2.3 Humpty's second look (after his great fall). This is a second puppet, identical to the first except for a few minor alterations

your construction process, but is much easier than attempting to change costumes during the performance.

Here, the character of Humpty Dumpty is created from a large plastic Easter egg ornament, with the elements of his clothing (along with his arms, legs, and facial features) attached permanently to his body. The only disadvantage to a permanent costume (especially if you've glued your seams) is that it cannot be changed easily if you decide you need to make any repairs or alterations later, and attempting to remove its costume could damage your puppet. This isn't a problem, however, if your puppet only has one role to play, and you can always add small accessories such as hats, glasses, etc. to change your puppet's look if needed.

Figure 2.4 A fish character named "Fin." This costume originally started out as a teddy bear's military uniform. The insignia was removed, a school crest was added, and other minor alterations were made to turn it into a school uniform. *(Fin appears courtesy of Grey Seal Puppets)*

Using store-bought clothing

Although most hand-made puppets will likely require their own custom clothing to ensure a proper fit, it is many times possible to find store-bought clothing that will work very well for the costume you're creating. Baby/children's clothing, and especially doll and teddy bear costumes, are available in a wide variety of sizes and styles, although you'll probably still need to make adjustments to fit your puppet. You'll also want to buy several sets of an outfit at the same time, in case you need extra fabric to make your alterations, or for repairing/rebuilding the costume down the road. It's often very hard to find the exact same outfit later on!

One item of store-bought clothing that's particularly useful is a man's or boy's collared button down shirt. Even if the shirt doesn't fit your puppet as it is, the front and collar can be cut off (serge or zigzag the cut edges to finish them) and attached to your puppet's body. You can then hide the cut-off "bib" under a sweater or coat. The cuffed sleeves of the shirt can also be cut off and used in this manner. This is a quick and easy way to give the illusion of a button-down shirt without having to alter the whole garment.

Another "shirt trick" is to use the top ribbed edge of a tube sock to make a great mock turtleneck. Cut the sock foot from the cuff, slit it up both sides to create a front and back, and pull it over your puppet's head. As with a button down collar, the cut edges can be hidden under an over garment such as a coat.

Altering store-bought clothing to fit will mainly involve trying the outfit on your puppet and making any adjustments; taking in or letting out seams, raising/lowering hems, marking where to cut an opening for a tail, etc. (If your alterations turn out to be too complicated, however, you're probably better off making the garment from scratch!). The alterations will be even easier if you're able to find an outfit that's already close to your puppet's size. Since baby's and children's clothing can vary from brand to brand, I recommend first

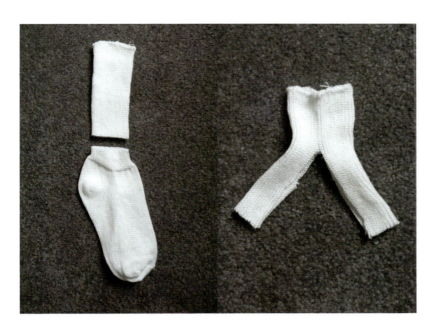

Figure 2.5 To create a mock turtleneck for your puppet, cut the ribbed cuff from an old sock, slit it up the sides, and pull the cuff over your puppet's head

Figure 2.6 Herbert wearing a sock mock turtleneck

measuring your puppet (its "chest," "waist," arm length and leg length), and taking both your measurements and your tape with you as you shop. That way, you can measure any appropriate clothing you find and make certain it will fit as close as possible. (If you're feeling especially ambitious, you can even try taking your puppet with you, to try on clothing as you shop!) Below is a basic chart you can follow to give you an idea of what size clothing to start with.

Table 2.1 Children's size chart (all measurements in inches)

	Newborn	6 months	12 months	2 years	3 years	4 years	5 years	6 years	7 years	8 years	10 years
Chest	up to 18	up to 20	up to 22	21	22	23	24	25	26	27	28.5
Waist	18	19	20	20	20.5	21	21.5	22	22.5	23	24
Hip	19	20	21	22	23	24	25	26	27	28	29
Sleeve (underarm to wrist)	6	6.5	7.5	8.5	9.5	10.5	11	11.5	12	12.5	13.5
Head	15	15	16	17	18 and up						

Note: Courtesy of The Fiber Gypsy, Children's Body Measurements and Garment Sizes, www.fibergypsy.com.common/children.shmtl

Doll and bear clothing, like children's clothing, also come in several standard sizes:

Table 2.2 Doll and bear size chart (all measurements in inches)

	Bust	Waist	Hips	Shoulder to waist	Waist to ankle
Barbie	5–5.5	3.25–3.5	4.75–5.25	3.5	6.5
15" Gene	6.34	4	6.34	4.5	8.5
15" Disney princess	7.5	7.25	9.25	4.5	7
18" American girl	11	10.25	12	5.5	9
17" baby doll	11.5	12	12.5	4.5	7.5
18" baby doll	12	11.5	13	4.5	8.5

Note: Courtesy of C.C. Originals, Doll Body Measurement Size Chart, www.ccoriginals.com/imagesdoll-bodymeasurmentssizechart.html and Helen B. Wharton, Bella Online, http:www.bellaonline.com/articles/art50945.asp

There may be other alterations needed to adjust store-bought clothing, such as creating an opening for the puppeteer's hand. This is something you'll need to take into consideration when you make your own costumes, and will be discussed further on.

Things to consider when costuming...

...Marionettes

The most important factor to consider when costuming a marionette is, of course, the strings. When creating a costume for a string puppet, make sure you don't have anything such as buttons, bulky trims, or large fasteners that will catch on the strings. You'll also need to take note of where your strings are (generally the hands, feet, and the top of the head). Design your costume carefully! A completely removable costume can certainly work for a marionette, although you'll have to tie the strings after the puppet is fully dressed, and untie them again should you need to remove the costume itself. The costume should also be fairly loose-fitting, so as not to restrict movement at the joints.

Figure 2.7 Herbert as a marionette, all tied up

Figure 2.8 This distinctive uniform, a recreation of those worn in one Civil War regiment, distinguished the soldiers known as "Zoauves." *(Uniform worn by Frank Hernandez)*

Figure 2.9 A marionette recreation of a Zouave soldier. Here the costume, while made up of several distinctive pieces, is attached directly to the wooden block that forms the puppet's body, and captures the period line and style of the uniform without being overly detailed *(Marionette constructed by Cricket Bauer)*

For a costume with a closer fit, it's probably best not to have a complete, conventionally sewn outfit, as this can hinder the puppet's movement. In this case it's better to glue or stitch fabric directly on to the marionette. Depending on how the puppet was constructed, you may even be able to paint the body to look like clothing. Not only will this help keep the joints free, it will cut down on the weight of the puppet.

With this marionette, the body is constructed simply of a block of wood, with a painted gourd for the head. The under-part of the costume—the shirt collar and the under tunic and "skirt"—are constructed separately but are also permanently attached to the wood body and to the underparts of the costume. The arms and legs have no inner support—the hands are painted wooden ice-cream spoons attached to the end of the jacket sleeves, while the boots have a wooden inner dowel support for the legging, and are glued directly to the

2 Types of costumes

Figure 2.10 A close-up of the hand, constructed simply of a painted wooden ice-cream spoon

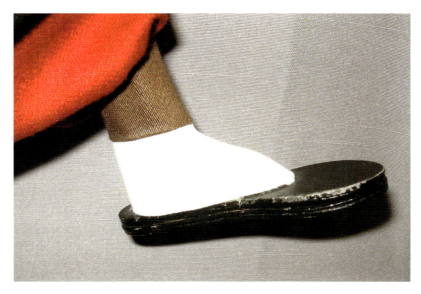

Figure 2.11 A close-up of the foot, also constructed of stacked and painted wooden ice-cream spoons

shoes (also wooden ice cream spoons). The fact that the marionette has nothing but the fabric of its costume acting as its arms and legs gives it a wide and flexible freedom of movement and helps keep the strings from getting tangled. In addition, although this costume is based on a historical military uniform and has many of the details associated with its larger counterpart, it is not overly detailed; the overall look and line of the uniform has been achieved without getting weighed down with the particulars, and still allows for good movement.

...Hand/rod puppets (and puppets with practical hands)

For this type of puppet, any one of the aforementioned costume types—store-bought, custom built, permanently attached or not—would work equally well. You will find that a hand puppet with a rod on one or both of the hands is, like a marionette, much easier to dress before the rods are attached. Depending on where the rods are attached to the puppet, the costume shouldn't need much work if any, to accommodate them.

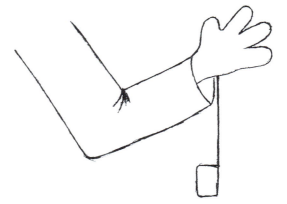

Figure 2.12 An illustration showing a hand puppet with a rod for manipulating its hands attached at the wrist. Here very little is needed in the way of altering a costume to accommodate the rod, although it is generally easier to dress the puppet before the rod is attached

A puppet with a practical hand will need more in the way of adjustments. Some practical hand puppets have a sleeve for the puppeteer attached at the wrist of the puppet; in this case you would not need to worry about enlarging the sleeve of the costume (although you might want to add some type of trim to the sleeve to camouflage the puppeteer's hand). Other puppets may have the puppeteer's hand coming in at the elbow, and the sleeves of a store-bought child's or doll's outfit may be too small for this. If you have enough matching fabric, you can enlarge and extend the sleeve by adding a piece of material to the end of the sleeve that is large enough for the puppeteer to get their hand through. Otherwise, you can create a sleeve of black or other neutral fabric to mask the puppeteer's arm.

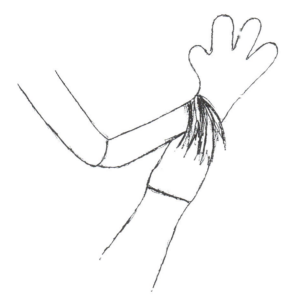

Figure 2.13 An illustration showing a "practical hand" puppet, where the puppeteer's hand emerges at the puppet's wrists and acts as the character's hand. Some type of camouflage, such as a lace cuff or other wrist decoration, may be helpful to complete the illusion

If you are constructing your own costume, be sure to make the sleeve large enough to accommodate the puppeteer. Leave an opening in the under forearm seam of the puppet's sleeve that will allow for the puppeteer's hand. Don't forget if you have multiple layers of clothing—a jacket over a complete shirt, for instance—to construct openings in the sleeves of both garments. Lastly, you'll want to create a sleeve going from the puppet's elbow of either fabric that matches the costume or of black/neutral fabric to mask the puppeteer's arm.

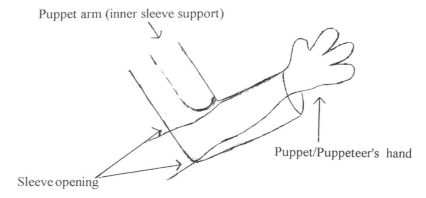

Figure 2.14 A "practical hand" puppet where the opening for the puppeteer's hand/lower arm is cut at the elbow of the puppet's garment. (The puppet's arm is bent purely for illustration purposes, and the puppeteer's sleeve used to mask the performer's arm attached to the elbow has been left off to show the placement of the opening)

...Hand puppets with legs

If your puppet is without legs, then only the suggestion of pants or a skirt is needed to complete the costume and hide the puppeteer's arm. You can alter a pair of store-bought pants for this by taking out the inseams of both legs and

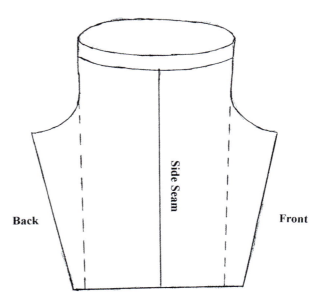

Figure 2.15 Constructing a pair of puppet "tube" pants from an actual pair of pants. Cut the stitching on both inseams, open them up, and re-stitch (right sides of fabric together) to form a tube, trimming away the excess fabric

stitching them together at the front and back to form a tube. A store-bought skirt should need no alteration other than the length of the hem if the waist already fits properly.

Some puppets, however, do have legs, and may need a full pair of pants. Store-bought pants should work very well with a minimum of alteration, especially if they already fit at the waist. You may need to adjust the hem, and open the center back seam from an inch or two below the waistband to the inseam, to accommodate the puppeteer. Similar adjustments will be needed when constructing your own pants, and the instructions for those, as well as how to make your own "tube" pants, are included in the next chapter.

chapter 3

Creating costumes for non-human puppets

In the past few chapters, we've discussed how to create costumes for puppets that are roughly people-shaped—that is, a head on a body with two arms and, occasionally, two legs as well. However, as mentioned in an earlier chapter, not all puppets come equipped with the standard extremities. While some puppets may have four or more arms and/or legs, some others may have none at all. Still others may have oversize wings or a tail that might need to be costumed around in addition to any rods or wires the puppet may have. Trying to build costumes around these can be challenging—particularly if you're attempting to alter existing store-bought clothing—but it's certainly achievable, and you can still create believable costumes without undue effort. Although it's not possible to anticipate *every* variety of non-human puppet, we'll give a few examples of different shapes, and hopefully spark ideas for you to costume your own oddly-shaped characters.

Costuming odd-shaped puppets (or those without arms and legs)

When costuming puppets with an odd shape—for instance, as in the found-object cone puppet pictured here—it is many times (although not always) easiest and most efficient to glue or sew the puppet's costume directly to its

Figure 3.1 A found-item puppet with a permanently attached costume (The Cone Puppet appears courtesy of Grey Seal Puppets, and is the father figure from an original piece by Drew Allison based on the song by Jimmy Buffet called "The Remittance Man")

Figure 3.2 Back view of The Cone Puppet. Here you can see the back seam of the fabric serving as his coat, glued into place

body. While not impossible to build an entire costume and then attempt to dress your puppet, it's generally not necessary. Quite often, simply gluing or stitching bits of fabric and trim to your puppet is all you need to create the illusion of a costume, and you can always "jazz it up" with accessories such as hair or jewelry. These types of costumes are likely to be permanent, as opposed to changeable—once glued, it can be difficult to remove the fabric or trims if you should change your mind later on. You can, however, change the overall look of the costume by simply changing the accessories if it becomes necessary to alter your puppet's appearance.

In the case of The Cone Puppet, his body base is a cardboard craft cone found at a hobby store, with a plastic toy baseball for his head. His costume was created by wrapping and gluing a scrap of suit fabric snugly to the cone itself, with another scrap of fabric cut and glued to create his shirt front. A black ribbon bow serves as his tie, while three black sewing pins, pushed into the bib front with a dab of hot glue on the inside of the cone to hold them in place, work well as buttons. His arms, cut from small lengths of cardboard tube, are covered from the same fabric as the body to complete the appearance of a suit jacket, and were costumed and attached as separate pieces on a wire to allow for freedom of movement. A plastic bead nose and scraps of fur glued to his head are all that is needed to give him a whimsical expression.

Another good example of an odd-shaped puppet is a familiar face from an earlier chapter—our old friend Humpty Dumpty. While the finished Humpty has

Figure 3.3 Humpty Dumpty

Figure 3.4 The starting point for Humpty's body, a large plastic Easter egg lawn ornament purchased from a hobby store

arms and legs, he didn't start out that way; his arms and legs were built and costumed as separate pieces, and were then stitched directly to the body of his costume. Let's take a look at the various pieces that go into costuming our egg-shaped friend.

The head/face: To create the top "egg" portion of his body, an elastic Lycra fabric was simply stretched over the plastic egg without needing any darts or seams, smoothed into place, and glued directly onto the plastic. A scrap of fur was glued on for hair, and his face was drawn on to the fabric with a black marker.

The shirt: Humpty's shirt was created by draping pieces of fabric on the egg, taking in darts/seams as needed, then gluing them directly on to the body. The collar was created separately from contrasting fabric, and also glued into place.

The pants and belt: As with Humpty's shirt, the fabric for his "pants" was draped on the lower half of the egg, stitched to fit, and also glued directly to the plastic. His belt is simply a strip of fabric with the edges turned/stitched to the desired width and then glued into place to cover the join between the shirt and pants. A decorative trinket serves as the belt buckle.

Lastly, as with the cone puppet, Humpty's arms and legs were created and costumed independently of his main body. Tubes of fabric stuffed with Polyfill were used to form the arm/leg structures; these were then covered in matching shirt/pants fabric to finish the look of the costume. In Humpty's case, once the main body of his costume was created, his arms and legs were then stitched directly to his costume to complete the puppet. However, the basic technique used here—gluing/stitching fabric directly to the puppet's form—can be used equally well to costume any puppets that are an unusual shape, and/or won't have arms or legs.

Figure 3.5 The main body of Humpty's costume, completed before the arms/legs are attached

While draping/gluing fabric pieces directly to your odd-shaped puppet can often be the easiest and most

3 Creating costumes for non-human puppets

efficient way of creating its costume, it's certainly not the sole method. Depending on the shape of your puppet, it's not impossible to sew a separate, almost-complete costume with which to dress it, as with the chicken characters pictured here. Unlike Humpty, which was a puppet made from an existing hard plastic shape that made gluing his costume to him more practical than stitching it, these puppets were custom made of soft foam and a "skin" of white fleece fabric that could be easily sewn to. Also unlike Humpty, whose head and body was one complete piece, these puppets have a head and body independent of each other; the body is a simple foam tube covered with fleece, with the head created as a separate piece to allow for maximum movement. Their costumes, while

Figure 3.6 Chicken puppets without extremities of any kind. Here, the head and body of the puppets are independent of each other to allow for head movement; their costumes are created as separate pieces and are stitched, not glued, directly to their bodies *(Chicken puppets designed and created by Grey Seal Puppets for Bojangles' Restaurants Inc.)*

Figure 3.7 Side view of boy chicken, showing the shirt and start of the overalls pattern. The shirt was created as a simple tube with a contrasting band for the "collar" and stitched directly to the puppet's body. The pattern for the overalls was created by draping fabric over the puppet's body, with the closure positioned at center back, and marking where the "arm openings" and "shoulder straps" should fall

Figure 3.8 Side view showing the finished shirt and overalls detail. The shoulder strap was created as a separate piece and stitched to the main body of the overalls, with a "buckle"/button and decorative contrast stitching added for realistic detail

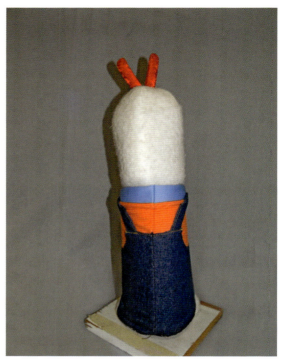

Figure 3.9 Back view of puppet, showing the center back closure hand-stitched together once the costume was completed and fitted to the puppet. Both shirt and overalls were then stitched directly to the puppet's body

draped on the puppet bodies to create the pattern in the same method as for Humpty, were built almost in the manner of real clothing—once the patterns for the individual pieces (the boy's shirt and overalls, and the girl's dress) were drafted, each item was constructed completely as a separate piece, then stitched to the fleece skin. The overalls were particularly challenging in that it was difficult to create an over-the-shoulder strap pattern for a puppet without any shoulders! However, once the pattern shape and placement were established, the final garment construction was fairly straightforward, and gave the illusion of a set of overalls, complete with shoulder straps.

Now that we've examined some methods of costuming odd-shaped puppets with only a few or no arms/legs, let's take a look at how to costume puppets that may have numerous arms/legs, such as the spider pictured below.

Costuming puppets with multiple limbs

Figure 3.10 A stylized spider puppet with six legs

This fellow is particularly challenging to costume—not only does he have six legs, he also has a face that covers the majority of the front of his body, making it difficult to create a believable costume around it. However, with a little patience and effort, you can create a costume using many of the same techniques used for the other odd-shaped puppets in this chapter. Let's see what can be done in the way of a tailcoat for our multi-legged puppet.

As with the cone puppet and Humpty, you'll find it easiest to create the body and the sleeves of the coat as separate pieces. Start by draping the fabric directly against the spider's body to begin creating the pattern for the main body of the jacket; again, this may prove tricky considering the shape of his body, the size of his face, and the number of legs involved. However, here we can pin the fabric straight into the body and legs to help hold it in place when marking the leg openings, seams, and front closure.

Remember that, for most puppets, intricate details aren't as important as the overall line of the costume. It will make constructing the costume much easier if you keep your pattern simple! A basic curved collar—created as a separate

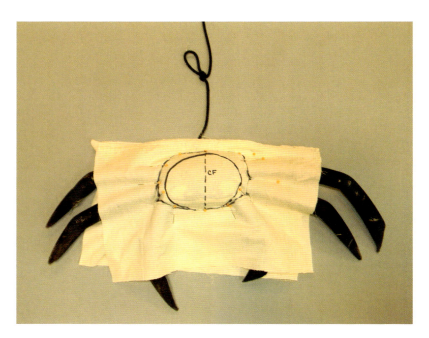

Figure 3.11 Draping the start of the base costume—front

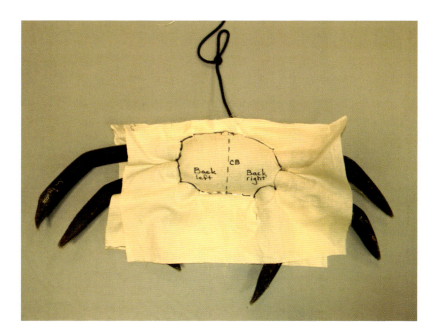

Figure 3.12 Draping the start of the base costume—back

3 Creating costumes for non-human puppets

Figure 3.13 Front opening cut away, and separate pattern piece for the collar pieces that can be constructed

Figure 3.14 The back of the draped muslin, showing the separate coat tail pieces

piece stitched to the edge of the front jacket opening—will give the general idea of a period coat collar without getting overly complicated. You can always add buttons or jewelry pieces to the finished garment as an easy means of adding interest to the overall costume.

The back coat tails, like the collar and sleeves, are most easily created as separate pieces and then attached to the basic coat.

Once you've completely draped your puppet, you can mark where any openings and seams will fall, and make any adjustments as needed. You can also at this point determine which seams you'll be able to stitch by machine when constructing the garment, and which may need to be left open so that you can dress the puppet once the costume is sewn together. In this case, it appears we'll be able to create a front and back for our costume and machine-stitch them along the top edge, leaving the sides and bottom open to be hand-stitched together once the puppet is dressed. (Make certain you leave a small opening in your top seam to allow for the puppet's string.)

Now that we have our pattern worked out, let's begin to build the coat!

To create the front of the jacket, it will likely be easiest to start by building the collar first, and incorporating that into the front of the jacket. Start by cutting a piece of fusible interfacing from your collar pattern (no seam allowance on the interfacing), and stitch around the outer (notched) edge, leaving the inner edge

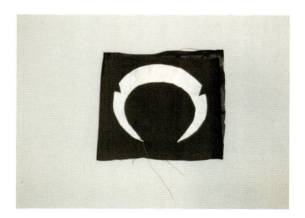

Figure 3.15 Starting to construct the collar. Here you see the interfacing fused to the wrong side of the collar fabric (in this case, black satin) before being stitched

Figure 3.16 The finished collar. The outside edges are finished, while the inside edge is left open, with ample seam allowance added to allow it to be stitched to the front of the coat

3 Creating costumes for non-human puppets

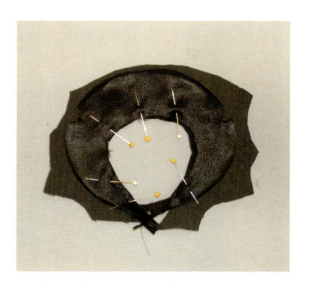

Figure 3.17 The front jacket pieces, with the finished collar sandwiched in between, before being stitched along the inside curved edge

Figure 3.18 The finished front. The two front jacket pieces can now be treated as one piece when being stitched to the back

open. Trim around your stitching, clipping the corners and into the notched edge; turn and press.

Once your collar is complete, you can then proceed to cut out *two* front jacket pieces from your draped pattern, making certain to include ample seam allowance. You'll then sandwich your collar in between these pieces, stitch along the inside edge, and turn and press to create a clean finished edge for the front of your jacket.

After you have completed the front of the jacket, you can then cut out the back (you only need one of the back, and again, don't forget your seam allowance!). Stitch the front and back pieces together at the top edge, making certain to leave a small opening in the seam to pull the top string through. Once you have stitched the front and back together to create the body of the coat, you can then dress your puppet and hand stitch the coat closed along the bottom edge, leaving the sides open.

3 Creating costumes for non-human puppets

Figure 3.19 The top machine-stitched edge of the spider's coat. Notice the opening left for the string

Figure 3.20 The bottom edge of the opening, hand stitched into place (and stitched directly to the puppet itself)

3 Creating costumes for non-human puppets

Figure 3.21 To create the sleeves, stitch tubes of matching fabric of a width and length to fit loosely on the puppet's legs. If you wish to create a cuff, add a strip of matching (or even contrasting fabric) to the end of the sleeve fabric before stitching the length of the tube closed to create the sleeve

Now that the base of the coat is in place, you can create the sleeves as simple tubes of matching fabric, adding a cuff if you wish. Cut the sleeve to the correct length, dress the legs, and hand-stitch them to the leg openings of the coat. You can also add buttons or other decorations to the sleeves if you wish.

Lastly, cut fabric for the coat tails from your pattern, and stitch two (a right and a left), turning them right-side out and pressing. Once completed, stitch the coat tails to the back of the jacket to complete the garment. You can also at this point add any final details you may desire, such as buttons or a hat, to complete the ensemble.

Figure 3.22 The finished tail coat (front), showing the attached sleeves

Figure 3.23 The finished tail coat (back), showing the tails and button detail

Altering store-bought clothing to fit odd-shaped puppets

In most cases with puppets that have an unusual shape or number of limbs, it truly is easier to create a custom garment from scratch, rather than try to alter an existing garment to fit. However, many times it's quite possible to use parts and pieces of ready-made clothing to build an original costume that will work well for your oddly shaped puppets. Some ideas for using store-bought clothing include:

- If creating a suit coat for a puppet with no arms—such as the chicken puppets shown earlier—you can alter an existing suit coat to fit by simply removing the sleeves and stitching the armholes closed, and/or taking in the side seams to fit.
- The collar and front button closure of a button-down shirt can be cut away and used to create a shirt-front (worn under a suit coat, like the one mentioned above).
- Coat and/or shirt sleeves can be cut from existing garments and used when costuming a multi-legged puppet—simply buy enough multiples of

the same outfit to procure the number of sleeves you need. You can use the remnant of the matching shirt/coat fabric to custom-make the base of your puppet's costume.
- And of course, store-bought doll and/or children's accessories—hats, jewelry, glasses, etc.—can very often be used as is, no matter what the shape of your puppet!

Creating costumes for oddly-shaped puppets doesn't have to be any more difficult than being patient and adding a dose of creativity. It can also be more fun!

chapter 4

How to create and construct basic patterns

Now that you have an idea of the basic construction procedures and know what type of costume will work best for your puppet, you can start to think about the patterns for your costume. There are several basic garment forms you can use as a starting point to create almost any type of costume imaginable for your puppet. These patterns are all included at the back of the book, with instructions on how to put them together in this chapter. As with the sewing techniques, the patterns will become familiar to you once you construct a few costumes.

How to use the patterns in this book (and how to do the photocopier trick)

All the patterns in this book are intended for puppets that are roughly "people-shaped." They can be used as they are, or scaled up or down in size in order to fit the particular puppet you are costuming. There is a very complicated mathematical process you can use to do this (and/or expensive computer programs used by professional pattern makers); for the purpose of our small puppet costumes, though, there's a technique we use that we like to call the "photocopier trick". This involves using the enlarge/reduce feature on a photocopier to scale your pattern up or down. The advantage to this method as opposed to just adding/subtracting inches from your pattern) is that the entire pattern will be scaled up/down proportionately. The disadvantage is that it can sometimes be very trial-and-error—it may take several attempts before you achieve just the right size for your pattern. There is a way that you can scale your pattern to fall within a general desired size range and cut down on the number of attempts you may have to make; here's how you do it.

In order to determine if you need to alter the size of a pattern, you'll first need to measure the dimensions of your puppet. The only measurement you'll need in order to use the basic patterns in this book is the widest part around your puppet. For a shirt/top, this will be the chest or waist, whichever is largest; and for pants or a skirt it will be the waist or hips. Compare these measurements to the width of the printed patterns to see if you'll need to scale your pattern up or down.

Next, photocopy your pattern, using the enlarge/reduce feature to scale your pattern to the size needed. The copier will do this by percentages, not by inches/centimeters; you might need to make several copies to get the size you need. However, there is a general formula you can use to bring your pattern to a certain size range.

Take the size in inches that you want your pattern to be. Divide that by the current size of your pattern, then take the resulting product and multiply that by 100. The end product will be the percentage needed to reduce or enlarge your pattern. The formula looks like this:

> "Size wanted" divided by "current size" = "scale factor" times 100 = the percentage needed to reduce or enlarge.

For example, if your puppet's waist measures 12 inches, and you need to enlarge a 4 inch pattern to fit, here's what you do:

> 12" divided by 4" = 3 × 100 = 300%. So, you'll want to enlarge your pattern by 300%.

If you need to reduce the pattern—for instance, if you need to scale the 4 inch pattern to fit a puppet with a 2-inch waist—the formula works this way:

> 2" divided by 4" = 0.5 × 100 = 50%. Here you need to reduce the pattern by 50%.

If you are making your pattern *really* large, you might need to photocopy several different areas of the pattern as you enlarge it, since it might not all fit on the same piece of paper. You can then cut out your pieces and tape them together to form your pattern. Once you've scaled your pattern to the correct size, you can then go on to make any adjustments and alterations you need. (None of the patterns in this book have seam allowances added, to allow for properly scaling up or down. You can add seam allowances later as you make your alterations.)

One thing you will probably want to do after you've completed your pattern is to make a *mock-up* of the garment you're planning to construct. This is basically a "trial run" of your garment to do an initial fitting on your puppet, and can be made of craft paper or scrap fabric. If you construct your mock-up from craft paper (for a simple garment such as a vest, for example), simply trace around your pattern pieces, cut them out, and tape them together (you won't need to worry about adding a seam allowance in this case). If, however, you want to make your mock-up from fabric, be sure to add a stitching allowance to your pattern for any seams that will be sewn together, and follow the instructions listed further on for putting your particular garment together (there's no need at this point worrying about the lining, hem, etc.—that won't come until you start constructing the actual garment). Once you've constructed your mock-up, you can try it on your puppet to test the fit of the costume, making and marking any alterations as needed to ensure a good fit. This will also let you see where in your costume you'll have to make allowances or create openings for any strings, rods, and/or hand openings your puppets has. Sometimes, depending on the type of costume you're trying to create, it may be easier to adjust the puppet instead of the costume!

Making a mock-up

Step 1: Start with your paper pattern, whether it's store bought or one that you've made by tracing the outlines of your puppet.

Step 2: Fitting the pattern to your puppet. Here you can make any changes needed to assure a good fit, such as taking in/letting out seams and marking your front and bottom edges.

Step 3: Once you've made the necessary adjustments, cut the fabric following your pattern. In this case, there is no seam allowance added to the pattern, and

4 How to create and construct basic patterns

Figure 4.1 The basic paper pattern

Figure 4.2 Adjusting the paper pattern on your puppet

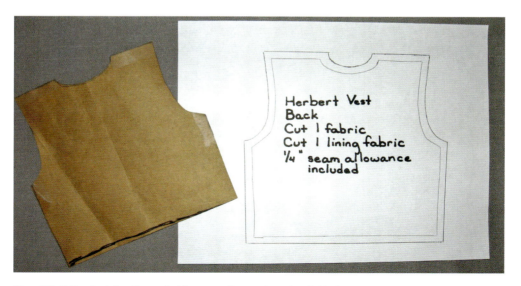

Figure 4.3 Making final alterations and adding seam allowance to create a finished paper pattern

4 How to create and construct basic patterns

you will need to take that into consideration when you are cutting and stitching your garment together. You can either trace around your pattern directly onto the fabric and stitch on your tracing line after you've cut your garment piece, or you can measure off a desired seam allowance from the stitching line and cut along that edge. I usually add a ¼" seam allowance to small patterns; commercial clothing patterns generally have a ⅝" seam allowance built in.

Finally, after you've finished your patterns, label them *immediately*, making notes as needed. Keep all your pattern pieces together in a labelled envelope for future reference.

Constructing the patterns

Shirt/bodice with sleeve

This is the pattern you will probably use the most in constructing your costumes, and is the first listed in the pattern section at the back of the book. With a little alteration, this basic pattern can be turned into a shirt, a vest, a coat, a dress, a robe—the possibilities are limited only by your imagination!

Once you've made the desired adjustments/alterations to your pattern, you can start putting it together. It may seem like a lot of extra work at the beginning, but it is usually better to put a lining in this type of garment. This makes it much easier to turn and create a clean finished edge on those tiny neck and arm holes. It can also save you the final step of having to hem the front and bottom edges of your garment. A lining will add strength and durability to your costume, as well as give it a more professional look. Remember, good workmanship is always important!

Here's a quick and easy way to construct your shirt/bodice:

Cut out your front and back pieces in both fabric and lining, making sure to add seam allowances if you haven't already done so on your pattern. Depending on whether you've designed your costume to have a front or back opening, you'll want to cut both a left and a right front/back. You will also need to add extra seam allowance to the edges of your opening (generally no more than ½") to allow for your closure. Velcro is the quickest and easiest type of closure, although you can also use snaps or a zipper if you're feeling truly ambitious! You can also hand-stitch the costume closed if it is meant to be permanent—

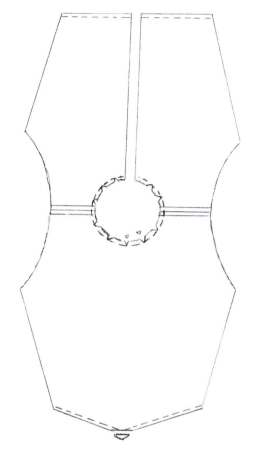

Figure 4.4 Constructing the basic bodice

no sense going to all the trouble of a closure if the costume will never be taken off and/or changed.

After you've cut your pieces, pin the shirt/bodice front and back at the shoulder seams (right sides together) and stitch. Do the same with your lining pieces.

Next, pin the bodice and lining (again, right sides together) and stitch around the neck opening and down the center front/back. Clip the curves of the neck opening (being careful not to clip your stitches!), turn the fabric right sides out, and press. If you want, you can then baste the bodice and lining together around the open edges so that you can treat it as one piece; this will make it easier to attach your closure and stitch the bodice to a skirt, if needed, or to pants if your garment is a shirt.

If you are creating a bodice with a dropped pointed waist (known as a "basque" waist), it is often easier to stitch along the bottom front and back edges along with the neck opening and closure, clip any points, and turn and press your bodice as above. This gives you a clean, finished bottom edge that you can trim easily, and one that fits nicely over a separate skirt and pants.

We'll discuss adding the sleeves a little further on.

Vest

To make a costume from the vest pattern printed in the back, cut the pieces as you would for a basic shirt/bodice, altering the bottom edge as desired (for instance, many vests come to a point at the bottom hem on both sides) and add extra width at the center front for overlap to create a vest closure. Stitch the pieces together following the instructions above, *and* stitch the armhole fabric and lining together just as you stitched the neck and front/back. You can also stitch the bottom hem; this will give you a nice finished edge at the bottom of your garment after you've turned it inside out. Leave the side seams open to pull the vest through as you turn it right sides out; once you've turned and pressed the garment, you can then stitch the side seams together. Add decoration as desired, such as buttons or trim.

4 How to create and construct basic patterns

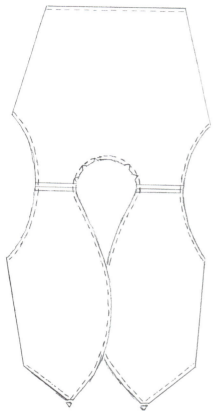

Figure 4.5 Constructing the vest

Figure 4.6 Herbert with his finished vest

Robe or dress

Cut fabric from the "robe" pattern as you would for a basic shirt/bodice, adding the "robe extension" piece to lengthen the hem as desired. Stitch the pieces together following the instructions above.

Once you've finished stitching your bodice and lining together, you can attach the sleeves. There are a wide variety of sleeve types you can use—a gathered sleeve can be for a dress or a pirate shirt, a close fitting sleeve would be better for a boy's shirt, the elongated sleeve works well for a wizard's robe. It is generally much easier to add any decoration on your sleeve before you attach it to the garment; it's also easier to hem it at that point, if you already know the finished length of your sleeve. You can do this by simply turning and stitching the bottom edge (see instructions for creating a hem in Chapter 1). Or you can create an elasticized edge or cuff that allows for easy changing, if needed, in a couple of different ways:

1. To create an elastic casing at the bottom of the sleeve, turn up the bottom edge approximately ⅜" (make sure the edge isn't left raw, or it will fray). Cut two pieces of ¼" elastic about three quarters the width of your sleeve. Thread the elastic through each sleeve casing, making sure to stitch the ends of the elastic and sleeve casings together at both ends of the sleeve to securely to anchor them.

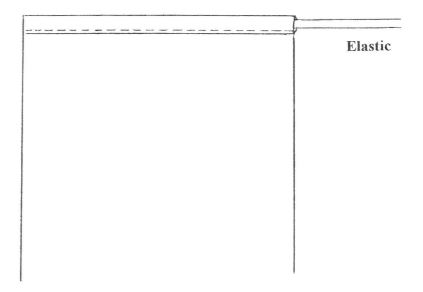

Figure 4.7 Elastic casing which can be used for a sleeve or pants/skirt waistband

2. For a ruffled edge at the bottom of your sleeve, draw a line lightly with a pencil or disappearing marker on the wrong side of the sleeve fabric, approximately 1" from the finished edge of the sleeve (this can be more or less depending on how big a ruffle looks right for the size of your puppet). Again cut 2 pieces of ¼" elastic three quarters the width of your sleeve. Secure one end of the elastic with several straight stitches to the sleeve fabric at your stitching line. Using a zigzag stitch wide enough to just catch

the edge of the elastic, sew the elastic down your stitching line, pulling the elastic tight and ruffling the fabric as you go. Secure the elastic at the end of the sleeve fabric with several straight stitches.

Figure 4.8 How to create a ruffled sleeve. Stitch lace to the hem of the sleeve before zigzagging elastic in place

After you've finished your sleeve treatment, you can attach it to the bodice. To do this, run two rows of gathering stitches along the upper edge of the sleeve and pull them to ruffle the fabric. Placing the right sides together, stitch the sleeve to the armhole of the garment.

Figure 4.9 Gathering the sleeve cap before attaching the sleeve to the bodice

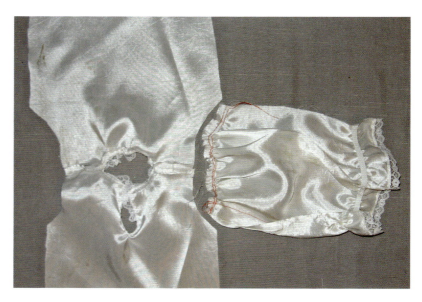

Figure 4.10 Attaching the sleeve to the bodice

Finally, you can stitch the side seam and underarm seam to complete your basic garment. (For a sleeve that will accommodate a practical hand, be sure to leave an opening in your underarm seam large enough for the puppeteer's hand to get through, having first made sure the sleeve itself is large enough as well!) As mentioned earlier, you can use this basic pattern to create a variety of different garments. You can use the shorter pattern to create a dress bodice, shirt, or top; you can attach the bodice to a skirt to create a dress; you can lengthen the pattern for a robe; you can add a lapel as with the spider tailcoat in the previous chapter to make a suit coat or jacket. After you've constructed the basic garment piece, you'll be ready to add any final decoration and/or closure, such as Velcro or snaps, to complete your garment.

Skirt

Creating a skirt is very simple, and can be completed in several different ways. We'll look at a few of the types of skirts that can be built, and how to go about creating them.

BASIC SKIRT WITH ELASTIC WAIST

For a this simple type of skirt, cut a rectangle of fabric approximately three times the waist measurement of your puppet by the desired length of your skirt, plus approximately an additional ¾" inch at the top/waist (this will be used to create a casing for the waist elastic). Stitch the lengthwise edges together to form a tube, and finish off the bottom edge as desired. Once the tube is complete, turn down the top edge of your waistband by about ¾" and stitch down to form the elastic casing, making certain to leave a small opening in your stitching to thread the elastic through. Cut a piece of ½" elastic, approximately the same length as your puppet's waist, and thread it through the casing, gathering the skirt fabric as you go. After you have run the elastic completely through the casing and back out of the opening, stitch both ends of the elastic together, and hand or machine stitch the casing closed to complete the skirt. This is a very simple garment to construct, and is especially versatile in that it can be easily dressed on or taken off your puppet.

GATHERED SKIRT WITH FITTED WAISTBAND

If you intend to attach the skirt to a bodice, or you will be adding a waistband to the top of the skirt, begin by creating the skirt tube as above, but *do not* stitch the entire length of the skirt's seam. Leave about 2" open at the top edge of the tube; this will make it easier to attach the bodice or waistband, and you

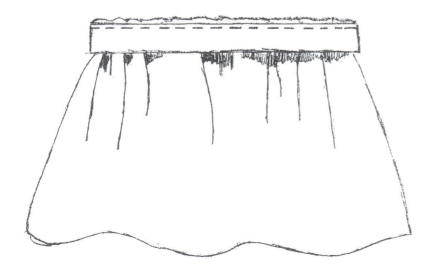

Figure 4.11 Creating a skirt with a gathered waistband

can add a closure later. For a skirt with a waistband, you'll want to first create the waistband itself by cutting a rectangle of fabric 2½" wide and the length of your puppet's waist measurement, plus two inches for seam allowance and a closure (this pattern allows for a ½" seam allowance all around). Fold the waistband in half and stitch the short ends closed; clip the corners, turn, and press to create a clean edge on each end of the waistband. Run a gathering stitch along the top edge of your skirt, and, right sides together, stitch the skirt to the waistband, leaving ½" overlap on each end. This should give you enough overlap to comfortably add a closure, such as a hook-and-eye, Velcro, or a snap, and you're done!

ATTACHING THE SKIRT TO A BODICE

The technique for creating a skirt that will be attached directly to a bodice, as opposed to having a gathered or fitted waistband, is exactly the same as described above, with the exception of having to build a separate waistband. Simply stitch your gathered tube skirt to the bottom edge of your bodice, add a closure or hand-stitch the opening closed, and you're done!

Variations on a theme: You can use this simple skirt pattern in several ways to create a variety of costume styles. Try stitching together several different-colored overskirts of lightweight, flowing fabric, such as chiffon, to make a full fairy princess skirt. Put a lace overlay, a half-skirt, or two separate side-pieces over your basic skirt for any number of historical styles. The possibilities are endless!

Pants

In the case of a hand puppet whose legs are never seen, the suggestion of pants can be created in much the same way as the tube skirt, although without the fullness and gathering at the waist. Cut a rectangle of fabric approximately the waist or hip measurement of your puppet (whichever is largest) by the

Figure 4.12 A skirt with an overlay made of contrasting fabric. Here both pieces can be constructed as separate "tubes," then put together and treated as one piece when creating an elastic or gathered waistband

desired length of the pants. Bear in mind that if the pants are serving as the puppeteer's sleeve, you'll want to make certain that they are long enough so that there is plenty of room for the puppeteer to manipulate it, without fear of the bottom of the pants accidentally showing above the play board and ruining the illusion. Also, be sure not to forget your seam/hem allowance! Add any decoration appropriate to the type of pants you're making (such as a satin stripe down the side for tuxedo pants, gold contrast stitching on denim for jeans, etc.). Stitch the ends together to form a tube, add a waistband (the same as for your skirt; if your puppet's waist is smaller than its hips, you will very likely need to gather the waist in just a bit), and you have a pair of pants!

For a puppet with legs, however, you'll want to construct an actual pair of pants, and the pattern for that is included at the back of the book. First, scale the pattern to fit your puppet (generally, scaling the waist/hip measurement of the pants to match that of your puppet will provide an adequate fit although creating a mock-up once you've altered your pattern is always a good idea).

To use the pattern included in this book, you'll want to cut four of the pattern pieces (two for each leg—be sure to flip your pattern pieces when cutting for right/left). Put two of your cut pieces right sides together and stitch along the straight edges on both sides (the long edge is your "outseam" and the shorter straight edge is your "inseam") to create a tube that will form one pants leg (do *not* stitch the top, bottom, or curved edge at this point). Repeat for a second pants leg. Turn one leg inside out so that the right side of the fabric faces outward, and place one pants leg within the other, lining up the curved edges (this will form the crotch seam of your pants) with right sides of the fabric together. Stitch along the curved edge, and turn your pants right-side out. Add a waistband (elastic gathered or straight waistband with the pants gathered into it—refer back to the skirt section if need be for instructions on how to do this), and hem the legs to complete the pants. You may also need to create an opening in the back of the pants for an arm sleeve for the puppeteer, although this is something that can be determined when you fit your mock-up. It may simply be a matter of leaving the back crotch seam open.

Once you've finished the pants, it's probably best to stitch them directly onto your puppet, if possible. This will ensure that they'll stay in place (imagine how embarrassing it would be to have your puppet's pants fall off in the middle of performance…). If your puppet has legs that can be taken on and off as needed, you'll want to be sure the pants can be changed as well. In this case,

Trick of the Trade

If you are adding any decoration or decorative stitching to your pants, such as a satin stripe for tuxedo pants or gold stitching on blue jeans it's much easier to do so before you completely construct the pants. Stitch the outseams of your pants legs together first, then press the seam open and leave the pants leg as a flat piece (do not stitch the inseam). Add your satin stripe or other decoration down the outseam, then finish constructing the pants as above.

putting Velcro on the waistband of the pants and on the puppet's waist will allow you to switch pants without worrying that you'll lose them at a crucial moment.

Cape

A cape is extremely simple to put together, and the pattern for creating a circle cape, both with and without a hood, is included in the patterns section at the back of the book. All that's needed is to scale it to fit your puppet, cut from your fabric and stitch the side seams, add any desired decoration, hem the bottom edge, and add a closure at the collar (such as ties, a hook and eye, or a button) to complete the costume piece.

By altering these basic patterns and combining them with interesting fabrics and accessories, you'll be able to construct almost any type of costume! After a little practice, you'll soon be able to easily determine just what alterations you'll need to make to your patterns to create the look you want.

chapter 5

Accessories

Once you've completed a costume for your puppet, you should consider what kind of accessories you'll want to go with it. Little things do mean a lot, and the right accessories can add the perfect finishing touch to your puppet's character. They can also give good clues to the type of role your puppet is playing. For example, round spectacles and gray or white hair could mean a grandmotherly type, while a red bandana and cowboy hat conjure up the image of a cowpoke from the Old West. As with clothing, you can often find doll or children's accessories that will work very well for your puppet with a minimum of alteration, and it's a great feeling when you come across that perfect hat or pair of glasses as you shop. It can be much more fun, though, to make your own! That way, you can be sure your tie or hat will match your costume perfectly, and it's really not as hard as you might think.

Wigs/hairpieces

One of the most important accessories you can give your puppet is hair and/or facial hair such as a mustache, beard, or eyebrows. Different hairstyles and facial hair can affect the shape of your puppet's head and face, and certain hairstyles are associated with certain types of characters. These, along with the types of material you choose for hair, as well as any hats or other headgear you might add, can complement your puppet's costume and define its character.

Figure 5.1 The opera singer Aida, a puppet in need of a hairstyle *(Aida appears courtesy of Grey Seal Puppets)*

There are a wide variety of materials you can use for your puppet's hair, and each has its own unique characteristics. Some good examples are:

- Actual wigs/hairpieces. You don't even need a complete wig or hairpiece to make a believable hairstyle for your puppet. Sometimes, you can use several different old hair pieces, such as those pictured here, to mix and match in creating just the right style for your puppet. It's often surprisingly easy to find different pieces that match in color.

Figure 5.2 A variety of hair pieces—a loose braid and cut pieces of various old wigs—that can be combined to create a single hairstyle

5 Accessories

Figure 5.5 The various pieces combined to give Aida the perfect opera singer hairstyle (front). One piece of old wig was stitched around her head to create the base of her hairstyle, with the braid wrapped into a bun and stitched to the top of her head to hide the "bald spot" left there. The curled pieces were stitched to the sides to add additional interest

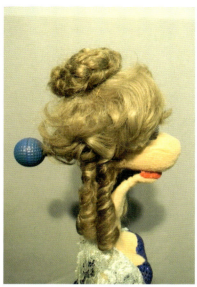

Figure 5.6 Aida's hairstyle (side)

Trick of the Trade

You can actually use the steam from an iron to help curl synthetic hair pieces. Begin by wrapping the hair around a cylindrical object, such as a dowel or pipe, and *lightly* steam the wrapped hair with an iron (don't get the iron too close, or the hair will melt!). Allow the hair to cool, then gently pull it from the dowel or pipe and spray the resulting curl with hair spray to help hold it in place.

Figure 5.3 Wrap synthetic hair around a dowel or pipe and lightly steam with an iron to curl it

Figure 5.4 The curled hair, compared to an uncurled piece

- Fabric. Experiment with cutting different types of fabrics into a fringe. Some stretchy fabrics such as polar fleece will curl nicely if you cut them and then pull the cut pieces.
- Fake fur. This also makes great beards, mustaches, and eyebrows. When cutting fake fur, use a razor blade or scissors to cut only the fabric backing, not the fur itself. This ensures your fur stays the same length. You don't want to cut it too short! Longer fur can also be neatly brushed and even set with hairspray to create a fashionable style.
- Feathers/marabou
- Chenille/crepe hair/doll hair (available at craft stores)
- And, of course, that good old standby, yarn. We'll talk more about how to make a great yarn wig later on.

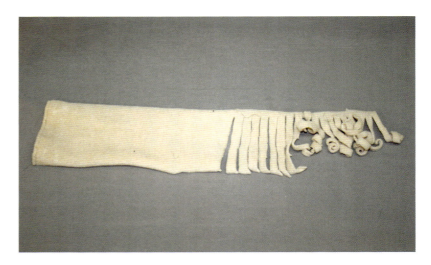

Figure 5.7 Polar fleece cut into fringe and then pulled to create a curly look

Trick of the Trade

When sewing fur pieces together, use a medium-to-wide zigzag stitch, brush the fur away from the edge, and stitch closely along the cut edge, allowing the far edge of the zigzag stitch to fall *over* the edge of the fur. This makes it easier to pull the fur out of the seam and disguise it.

Figure 5.8 Herbert with polar fleece hair

5 Accessories

Figure 5.9 Pom poms can make great colorful hair

Figure 5.10 Pipe cleaners can also make colorful hair, and can be bent to create a variety of styles

Look beyond standard hair ideas! You can also use:

- Raffia
- Cassette tape/cheerleading pom-poms
- Scrub brushes
- Pipe cleaners. Try winding these around a pencil to create curls
- Mops. Cotton mops can be cut from their poles and dyed different colors
- Broom straw

Hair construction techniques

While the easiest way to make hair for your puppet is to stitch or glue your chosen material directly on to your puppet's head, you may sometimes want a more finished look. Here are a few ideas for putting together puppet wigs.

Figure 5.11 A found-item puppet of Blackbeard the Pirate. Here Blackbeard's signature beard is a cotton-string mop cut from its handle and dyed black before being stitched to the puppet *(Blackbeard appears courtesy of Grey Seal Puppets)*

Stitched center-part wig

Although yarn is probably the most popular material for this type of puppet hairpiece, you don't have to limit yourself to it. You can also use different colors of cording, string, lengths of cassette tape, or raffia—use your imagination!

To make this type of wig, start by cutting even lengths of yarn twice as long as you want your puppet's hair to be (it's better to make the lengths longer than you think—you can always cut them later!). The easiest way to do this is to wrap the yarn several times around your hand or other object (such as a book) and cut all the strands along the same edge. Make certain to wrap the yarn loosely, though—if you wrap it too tightly the yarn will stretch and your hair will be shorter than you intended. Also, be sparing with how many strands you wrap, as too much yarn can make the wig very heavy.

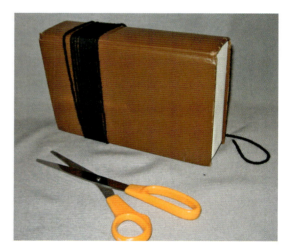

Figure 5.12 Creating lengths for a yarn wig

Next, cut a piece of ribbon the same length as your puppet's head from front to back, and lay the yarn evenly across the ribbon, making certain to center the ribbon on the strands (if you want, you can lay a piece of masking tape across the yarn to help hold the strands in place). Hand stitch the ribbon to the yarn (or you can run it through your machine if you're feeling ambitious), being careful to catch all the strands and creating a solid line of stitching. You may need to sew to the end once and back again to catch all the yarn. This forms the center part of your puppet's hair.

Figure 5.13 Close-up on the center part of a yarn wig, showing the yarn stitched on to a piece of ribbon

After you've completed the wig and removed the tape, you can braid it and/or cut it to create hairstyles for your puppet. Be very careful when cutting—remember, it won't grow back! Try adding ribbons or other accessories to jazz it up.

Glasses

Another great accessory that can add to your puppet's character is eyeglasses. Plastic or wire-frame glasses can be easily found at department or dollar stores in a wide variety of colors, shapes, and sizes (you can also poke out the lenses of sunglasses if you like the frames but don't want the dark "shades.") Doll or children's glasses work well, although larger regular-sized glasses can be very funny on a small-scale puppet. Try putting your puppet's eyes directly on the lenses instead of behind them, for a funny "bug-eye" effect.

You can also make your own simple pair of wire-frame glasses using an old coat hanger, or wire purchased from the hardware store. Cut and straighten your hanger (or cut a length of wire), mark the center of your piece of wire, then

Figure 5.14 Herbert sporting a center-part yarn wig, complete with bangs

Figure 5.15 Wire-rim glasses with the eyes placed directly on top, instead of behind the frames

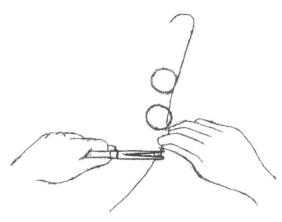

Figure 5.16 Simple wire-frame puppet-sized glasses can be created by bending wires into the appropriate shape

mark how wide you want your glasses to be. Use a pair of needle-nose pliers to bend the wire into either a rectangle or circle for each eyepiece. Bend the wire again at the sides to make the side pieces, then bend a small curve at end for the ears.

Jewelry

As with glasses, suitable jewelry can be found at department or even thrift stores. It doesn't even have to be in good condition. A broken necklace that may be too short for a person to wear could be the perfect size for your puppet, and can be sewn directly to your puppet's costume or body. Brooches, earrings, and rings can all be used to add to your puppet's overall appearance.

Think beyond actual jewelry. A pair of matching buttons could be a neat set of earrings, or a single large unusual button could make a handsome brooch, pendant, or ring. Metallic sewing trims can also be used as jewelry (a necklace, bracelet, or ring), while an elegant hair comb could be turned into a tiara fit for a princess.

Trick of the Trade

If your puppet is going to wear a necklace, be sure to tack it down in several spots on the puppet's costume or body, so that when you are putting the puppet on or taking it off, the necklace doesn't accidentally swing up over the puppet's head.

Gloves

Store-bought gloves might work for your puppet's costume, but only if your puppet actually has five fingers. You can, of course, cut a finger or two from a pair of gloves and then stitch the openings closed.

The best way to make well-fitting pair of gloves for your puppet is to trace around its hand onto a piece of fabric (preferably fabric with a stretch, such as a knit), and stitch on the tracing line.

Cut around the stitching line, turn the glove inside out, and add any decoration you might want.

You can also make mittens this way.

A piece of pretty edged lace, wrapped and stitched around your puppet's hand, works well as a lace mitt for a lady in period or evening clothes.

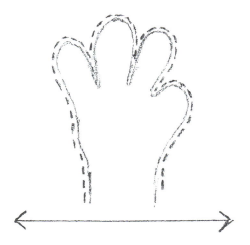

Figure 5.17 When creating gloves, trace slightly outside the outline of your puppet's hand and stitch along the marked line

Ties (and other neck adornments)

Ties are another great indicator of your puppet's character. A narrow, dark conservative tie would be suited for a business person such as a banker or lawyer, while a loud-colored tie would indicate a flashier character. Ties and other neck adornments such as scarves can also help hide any gap between your puppet's head and body. You can use small clip-on ties just the way they are—simply stitch them to the collar of your puppet's costume. You can also cut down larger ties to fit if you find a color and/or pattern that you like.

Or you can make your own tie! Using the tie pattern at the back of the book, cut two of the top tie pieces and one of the bottom tie pieces from the fabric of your choice (as with most puppet costume items, lightweight fabric works best). Be sure to add a seam allowance around your stitching line! With right sides of the fabric together, stitch the two top pieces together at the top and bottom edges, leaving the sides open (Figure 5.18.1). Clip the edges of the seam allowance, turn the top piece right sides out, and press. Stitch the sides together and turn again so that the raw seam edge is on the inside of the tie piece (5.18.2).

Figure 5.18 Steps for creating a custom tie

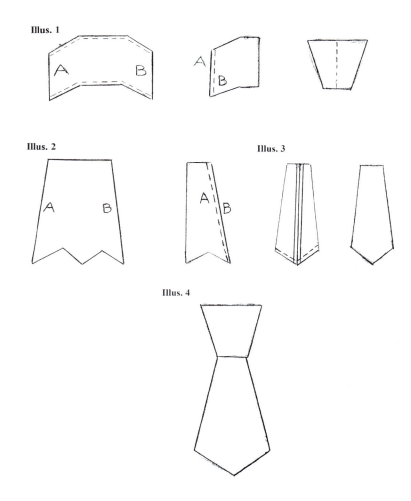

Next, stitch the long edges of the bottom tie piece (again, right sides of fabric together, then center the seam on the tie piece and stitch the bottom angled edge as shown (Figure 5.18.3). Clip the point of the tie and turn right-side out; press. Stuff the raw top edge of the long tie piece into the bottom opening of the top piece and finish with a few hand stitches (5.18.4). Stitch the tie to the collar of your puppet's costume and you're done!

Not all neckwear is quite so complicated. A plain square or triangle of fabric makes a great shawl, and can be used for a grandmotherly type, or a gypsy fortune-teller.

Shoes

If you're using hand or hand/rod puppets, then more often than not the lower half of your puppet's body will never be seen. In this case, shoes would not be a necessary part of your puppet's costume. However, there may be times when you *will* want shoes for your puppet, such as for marionettes, or if you're performing *Cinderella*.

Store-bought vs home-made shoes

Very often, purchased shoes (either doll or baby/children's shoes) will work well for your puppet's costume. The only drawback, though, is that real shoes can be very heavy. Also, if your puppet's foot is an odd shape, or you need a period shoe, you might not be able to find one in a store (although many times you can alter a modern shoe to look more period, such as adding a buckle or some jewels). In this case, you may want to custom make your own shoes.

When constructing a pair of shoes, there are certain basic techniques you'll use for almost every type of footwear your puppet could need. The pattern for creating a basic pair of shoes is included in the patterns section at the back of the book, and you can alter or embellish it to suit your puppet (use the photocopier trick to adjust your pattern to fit, using the length of your puppet's foot as the base measurement). Any decorative stitching you may want should always be completed before the shoe is assembled, and make certain to flip your patterns when tracing, to create both a right and a left shoe.

To create a pair of shoes

Using the shoe patterns at the back of the book, fit your puppet's foot to the sole pattern and make any needed adjustments in size (remember the photocopier trick! And don't forget to reduce/enlarge *all* parts of the pattern by the same amount).

Cut four soles from poster board or light weight cardboard (two right and two left). One pair will be your inner soles, and the other will become the outer sole.

Cut two shoe upper pieces from your chosen material (we'll discuss fabric choices further on). With the right sides of the material together, stitch the heel seam, and turn the uppers right-side out.

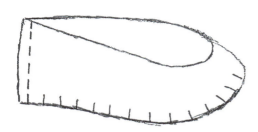

Figure 5.19 Once the center back seam of the shoe upper is stitched, cut ¼" into and around the bottom edge to create tabs

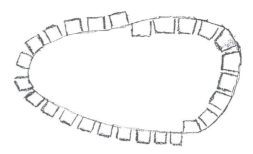

Figure 5.20 Fit one (inner) sole to the bottom of the shoe and bend the tabs inwards to glue along the bottom of the sole

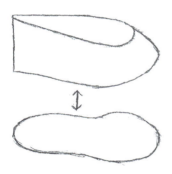

Figure 5.21 Glue the second (outer) sole to the bottom of the shoe, neatly covering the tabs and helping secure the glued edge

Cut ¼" slashes all the way around the bottom edge of the upper. Using hot glue, carefully fold and glue the slashed upper completely around the edge of the inner sole.

Glue the outer sole to the bottom of your shoe, pressing the soles together as tightly as possible to eliminate any space between them.

Decorate and enjoy!

When choosing materials for your shoes, you may be tempted to use leather or vinyl as in a real shoe. This is fine, but be aware that these materials can be difficult to work with on a small scale, especially thick leathers. If you *do* decide to use vinyl or real leather, go with as thin a material as possible—too thin is better in this case than too thick.

Some suggested materials and variations on a theme:

- Use clear vinyl to create glass slippers for Cinderella. Embellish the slippers with an iridescent rose, bow, and/or beads.
- Brown or tan felt works well as "suede" to create cowboy boots. Add some decorative stitching to the sides of your boot (remember, finish this stitching *before* you assemble the boot!), and add a felt boot strap at the back or sides. You can even create a heel (for this and other shoes) by tracing the back half of your shoe pattern onto thick cardboard, cutting out the heel, then painting it or covering it with matching fabric before gluing it to the shoe.
- Cut your shoe from black shiny vinyl and add a strap and buckle to create Mary Janes for Alice in Wonderland. (Want socks to go with them? Doll and/or baby socks work fine just the way they are.)

Trick of the Trade

When gluing leather or vinyl, mark off the area you plan to cement together, then use sandpaper to lightly scuff up the slick surface finish in that area before you apply the glue. This gives you a better surface area for the glue to adhere to.

You can also cut your shoe uppers from poster board and cover them with fabric to match or complement your puppet's costume. Cut the fabric slightly larger than your poster board upper and glue the fabric down with white craft glue, wrapping and securely gluing the edges of the upper. Instead of stitching your back seam, though, simply overlap the back edges of the fabric-covered upper and glue in place. Continue constructing as you normally would.

> **Trick of the Trade**
>
> If you have a thick leather or vinyl, it's easier to hand stitch if you mark your stitching line, then use a punch to make holes along your line that you can then stitch through.

Figure 5.22 Dorothy's ruby slippers, made by cutting the shoe upper from poster board and covering with red sequin fabric, then attaching the sole, a cardboard heel (also covered with red fabric) and a bow. The slipper is then "soled" with red felt

Hats and other headwear

Like other accessories, useful hats can often be found at department, thrift, or craft stores. As always, doll/bear and baby's or children's hats can work very well for your puppet. You can also find at craft stores straw hats or small hat forms that can simply be covered with fabric and/or decorated with flowers, ribbon, or other items. True millinery—the art of making hats—can be difficult especially if you're attempting a period look! However, there are a few basic patterns you can use, as well as a few construction tricks, to create a wide variety of simple but effective hats of your own. These patterns are included in the patterns section at the back of the book.

As with shoes, there are certain construction techniques and materials you'll use to create the beginning hat shapes. After that, all you'll need is a little alteration and embellishment.

The basic hat shape

Cut one each of your hat brim, crown, and side from poster board, buckram, or hat brim. (Buckram and hat brim are stiff materials especially intended for millinery. They can often be found at fabric stores.) Overlap the back edges of the side piece ¼" and glue into place. Cut ¼" slashes all the way around the edge of the crown; bend the edges down and glue them around the top edge of your side pieces.

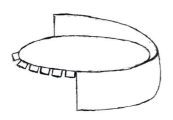

Figure 5.23 Attaching the hat side to the crown. Once the two pieces are glued together, cover with the fabric of your choice

At this point, you'll want to cover your finished top piece and the hat brim with your choice of fabric, and will use these same pattern pieces to cut out the fabric. Craft felt is a good choice for most hats, as it mimics actual hat felt and doesn't need finishing along the edges. Cut your fabric pieces slightly larger than the pattern pieces. Using a thin coating of white craft glue, secure the felt crown piece to the top of the hat, leaving a ¼" overlap around the edges. Slash into this overlap completely around the edge of the crown, fold the edges down, and glue into place. Wrap the fabric side piece around, lining the top edges up neatly, and glue down the overlap in the back.

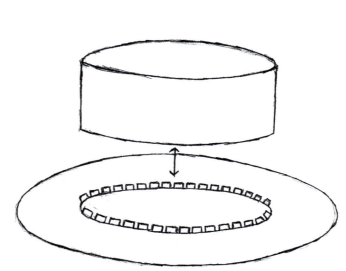

Figure 5.24 Attaching the hat side/crown to the brim

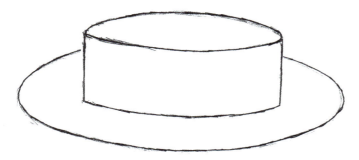

Figure 5.25 The finished basic hat

Cover your hat brim (again using a thin coating of white craft glue) and cut the head opening as marked on the pattern. Cut ¼" slashes all the way round the inside edge of the hat brim, and fold them up. Place the top of your hat on the brim with the folded up-tabs on the inside, and hot glue the tabs all along the inside edge of the hat top. You have a basic hat!

Variations on a theme: You can use this shape as the starting point for a multitude of different hat styles. For example:

- Elongate the side of the hat and cover with black felt to create Abraham Lincoln's signature stove-pipe hat. You can also add a satin ribbon along the bottom edge where the side piece meets the crown, and use gray or brown felt, to create a Dickens-style top hat.

Figure 5.26 The basic hat can easily be turned into a tricorn by folding up three sides and adding trim

- Create a hat base with a shorter height; cover with red or blue felt, glue gold trim along the edge of the brim, fold up one side, and stitch/glue in place. Add trim and a jewel or feather for a hat the Three Musketeers would envy. Or, using black felt and appropriate trim/decoration, fold up all three sides of the hat brim for a pirate's or soldier's tricorn.

So much for men's hats! Here are some for the ladies:

Basic bonnet

Pattern a circle that curves adequately over your puppet's head (see the photo of Herbert in the lady's bonnet, to get an idea of where the circle needs to fall on the head and how large it should be). Once you've patterned the circle, cut it from poster board or hat brim. Cover it with a fabric of your choice (you don't necessarily need to use felt for this type of hat, but you'll want to either use a fabric that won't fray, or make certain the edges are securely glued so your fabric won't unravel). Glue lace and/or trim all around the edge of the bonnet, attach a length of ribbon at each side to tie under your puppet's chin, and decorate as desired.

Figure 5.27 A basic lady's bonnet laid out flat. This is made by simply cutting a circle of poster board, covering it with fabric if desired, and trimming it with ribbon or lace

5 Accessories

Figure 5.28 The basic lady's bonnet on Herbert, looking much more like a hat once it's placed on an actual head!

Princess hat

Using the "pointed hat" pattern, cut your pattern piece from poster board or hat brim, and cover it with fabric. Overlap the back edges and hot glue securely into place. Add decoration, such as marabou or an elegant trim along the bottom edge, and a gauzy veil flowing from the top.

Variations on a theme: You can also use this pattern to create a hat for a wizard or clown, as well as use it for the standard witch's hat. Cut a hat brim in addition to the pointed hat piece, and cover both with black felt. Attach the pieces as instructed for the "basic hat shape."

Another simple hat shape that can be used for a variety of different time periods and fairy tales is the "mob cap." This is a simple circle of fabric gathered with a piece of elastic and ruffled along the edge. Cut the circle from a piece of muslin or white broadcloth, and

Figure 5.29 The "pointed hat" used to create a medieval princess hat

lightly trace a stitching line with pencil or disappearing marker 1" to 1½" inside the edge of the circle onto your fabric. Finish the edge, or stitch on a piece of lace.

Take a ¼" piece of elastic, wrap it snugly around your puppet's head, and cut the elastic to this length with just a small bit extra for overlap. Following the stitching line marked on your fabric, sew the elastic down using a wide zigzag stitch, keeping the elastic pulled tight as you go and gathering the fabric, until the elastic is sewn completely around.

Figure 5.30 Sewing the elastic to ruffle the mob cap

Figure 5.31 Herbert sporting the versatile mob cap

Variations on a theme: Try using a heavier, more ornate fabric with this pattern and adding a feather and jewel to create a Renaissance hat for your fairy-tale prince.

Other hat and headwear ideas

Use half a plastic craft sphere, or the round bottom of a large plastic Easter egg, as the basis for a baseball cap. Paint the piece or cover it with a stretchy fabric (so there will be no puckers!), cut and add a matching brim of colored ⅛" "Fun Foam" (found at craft stores), and glue a button to the top. You can also use this sphere or egg bottom as the round part of a derby hat—simply paint or cover it, then add a brim and decoration if desired.

You can make a king's crown by cutting a piece from a round plastic food container (such as a cottage cheese container). Cut a segment of the plastic container, snip points to create your crown base, and then paint and decorate it as desired. Or you can trace the pattern from the back of the book onto poster board or another stiff material, curve it into a circle to form your crown, glue it in place, and paint/decorate it.

A simple square of fabric, with or without trim along the edges, makes a nice head scarf. Tie it in place on your puppet's head with a decorative cord, and you have a burnoose for a shepherd or desert sheik.

There are hundreds of other accessory ideas you could use to complement your puppet's wardrobe, but these should be enough to help get you started. It won't be long before you develop an eye for just what types of accessories you need for your puppet, and what you can do to find and/or create them.

Figure 5.32 Cutting a crown shape from the bottom edge of a plastic container

chapter 6

Props

In previous chapters, we've discussed how your puppet's costume and costume accessories can play a large part in defining its character. While the main focus of this work is on costumes—the clothing and accessories worn by your puppet to create the appearance characteristic of its role—there are many instances where small hand props can be just as integral in helping define that role. Tiny Tim's crutch in *A Christmas Carol*, while not worn as an actual costume piece, is certainly an iconic part of his overall character presentation, and is just as important in defining his costume as his hat or scarf. In this chapter, we'll take a look at several basic hand props that can be used to enhance your puppet's costume, and that can give your audience additional information on its character.

Stage props (shortened from stage properties) are any movable or portable objects used on stage or screen by performers during a production. They are generally distinct from the actors, sets, and costuming, although as mentioned above there are certain types of props that are just as important to the performer's costume as the costume pieces themselves. Some of the different types of props are defined below; for the purposes of puppet costuming, you will really only need to focus on one or two.

Different types of stage props include:

Set props: Any props that "live" on the stage—in other words, objects that are part of the set that the performers use during the production. If your set involves a library, for instance, then it may have books that are used as **set dressing** (display) and other books that your puppet may actually pick up and use. Only the books that your puppet handles are considered props. Other types of set props may include drinking glasses, pens and pencils, cooking pots and pans, etc. These are not necessarily part of the costuming except that—depending on how your puppet will be picking up and manipulating the prop—you may have control and attachment mechanisms that you will have to take into consideration when designing and constructing the costume.

Figure 6.1 An example of a set prop. Here Herbert is in a library, reading a book. Only the book(s) that he actually uses are considered props; the rest are set dressing

Hand props: These are any objects that the performer carries with them onstage to use in their performance (as opposed to set props that are already on stage). Examples of hand props include Tiny Tim's crutch (as mentioned above), books, lanterns, letters, flowers, brooms, etc. Hand props can be an important part of your puppet's overall costume; for example, a witch character can be further defined by the addition of a broom.

Costume props: These can also be considered **costume accessories**, mentioned in the previous chapter. Costume props are any props that "live" on the actor's costume, and include such items as jewelry, eyeglasses, and hats. If the accessory is worn simply for decoration, then it is considered as part of the costume; however, if the puppet handles the piece during the performance, it is considered a prop. As has been discussed, these pieces can play an integral part in defining your puppet's character.

6 Props

Figure 6.2 A broom can be considered a hand prop if your puppet carries it on stage as it enters for its performance

Figure 6.3 Herbert tips his hat. Here, his hat, while technically a costume accessory, can also be considered a costume prop if he uses it during the performance

Practical props: A prop is considered practical if it actually has to function during the course of the performance. A lantern that must actually light, for instance, is a practical prop. As with set props, these may not necessarily need to be a concern with your puppet's costuming except with the logistics involved in the practical operation of the prop (such as running wiring for lighting, costuming around the attachment/manipulation controls, etc.).

As with many costume accessories, you can quite often find ready-made doll or bear props that will work perfectly well for your puppet, such as the backpack in Figure 6.4. Other doll and/or children's play items that work well are plastic tea sets, pots and pans, tableware, combs, brushes, and hand mirrors. There are also any number of craft, household, and novelty items that can make serviceable props for your puppet. Some everyday items that you might consider are:

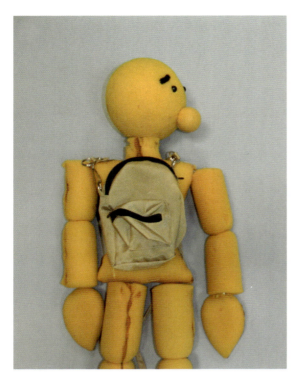

Figure 6.4 Herbert with a ready-made doll's backpack, ready for a hike!

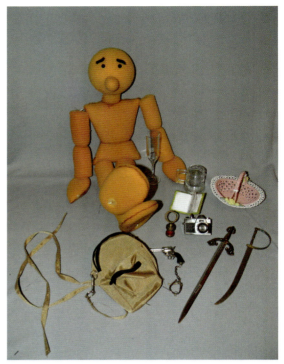

Figure 6.5 Some home and craft items that can work as puppet props

- Baskets, something that Little Red Riding Hood may need for her trip to Grandmother's house. These can be found in a variety of sizes and styles at craft stores.
- Party favors, such as small-scale plastic champagne bottles/glasses and hand fans.
- Novelty key chains and Christmas ornaments. You can often find these made as smaller recreations of larger everyday items, such as cameras.
- Golf pencils can be a good size for a small puppet hand (although regular pencils are often fine as well). Just remember that when using real pencils, markers, or pens to cover the point with something (such as a dab of glue) that will keep it from marking all over your puppet, its costume, and other show items.
- Decorative letter openers, which can serve nicely as a sword for a pirate or prince. Make certain, though, that they are light enough to use comfortably in a performance, and be sure to dull down any sharp edges or points!

A small plastic cocktail pick makes an excellent sword for a particularly tiny puppet.

Bear in mind, however, that even though you may want a smaller-size version of an item to be more in keeping with the scale of your puppet, in a live stage performance you will still want the prop to be visible to your audience. It may be just as effective, if not more so, to use a regular size plastic cup or plate with your puppet as it is to use a doll-size one (it can certainly be more comedic!). Just as the overall line of your puppet's costume is more important than intricate details in conveying information about its character, the general silhouette and color of any props may well be all you need for an effective performance.

Now that we have a general idea of the types of props we might be able to find ready-made for our puppet, let's create a few of our own from scratch! While it would be extremely difficult to cover every type of hand prop you might want or need for a performance, the previous and following examples should hopefully provide a few ideas on how to go about finding and/ or building the perfect prop for your puppet's costume.

Figure 6.6 Finger-puppet Herbert sporting a painted cocktail pick sword

Ladies' hand fan

While it is not unlikely you can find an appropriate fan at a craft or party store, they are extremely simple to make, and by creating your own you can be certain it will be the perfect size, color, and shape. These fans can be made from decorative paper, lightweight paperboard, or even stiff fabric, and further ornamented with tassels or and/or lace edging.

Step 1: Start by cutting a rectangle of paper or paperboard the approximate height you want your finished fan to be, and twice that measurement for its length (for the purposes of this illustration, a plain white paper was used, and cut to 4" high by 8" long).

Step 2: Lightly mark ½" increments along the length of the rectangle. Once you have completed your markings, it is at this point that you'll want to stitch or glue any lace or other desired decorative trim along the top edge of your fan.

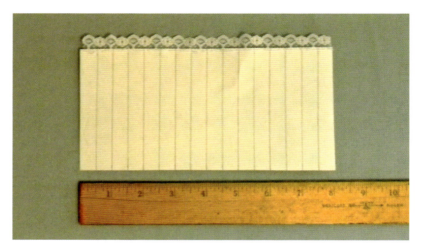

Figure 6.7 The start of a basic fan, showing the markings where the fan pleating will be rendered, and the decorative trim along the top edge

Step 3: Starting from one end, fold accordion pleats on your markings along the entire length of the fan.

Figure 6.8 Starting the accordion pleats on your fan…

Figure 6.9 …and the finished pleats

Step 4: Once the pleats are complete, pinch in the bottom end of your fan (about ½" from the bottom edge) and secure in place with a few hand stitches. Fan out the top pleats to form a nice rounded fan. You can add a decorative tassel or other ornamentation to the bottom if you wish.

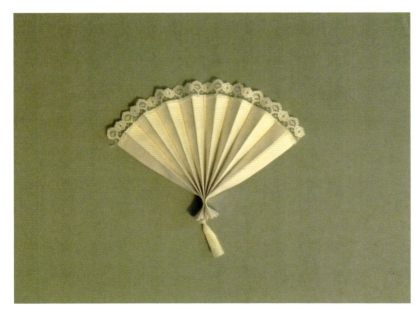

Figure 6.10 The finished fan

Drawstring Bag

Another good hand prop is a drawstring bag. These work equally well for both ladies' and men's accessories; depending on the materials used, a drawstring bag can serve as either a purse for an eighteenth-century lady, or a simple money pouch for a medieval peasant. There are several different ways to create a drawstring bag; we'll look at two of them here.

A simple pouch

Step 1: You'll first want to determine how large your pouch needs to be. Once you've determined its approximate size, you can then cut a square of plain fabric the finished height of your bag (plus approximately 1" for a bottom seam and drawstring casing at the top), by a width twice the finished measurement, plus ½" added for a seam allowance. For example, if you wish your pouch to be 4" × 4", you'll want to cut your piece of fabric 5" × 8½".

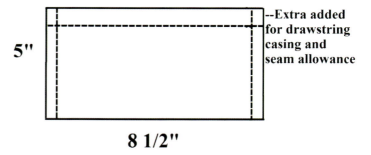

Figure 6.11 Cutting the fabric for a simple drawstring pouch

Step 2: Once you've cut your fabric, fold it lengthwise and stitch along the bottom edge and side at ¼". Leave a small opening at the top of the side seam that will accommodate the drawstring.

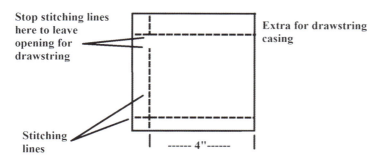

Figure 6.12 Folding and stitching the fabric to create the basic bag

Step 3: Turn your bag right side out. Fold the top edge approximately ½" down and stitch to form the drawstring casing.

Step 4: After the casing has been stitched in place, thread a drawstring through the opening in the side seam completely through and back out. You can knot both ends of the drawstring together, and pull tightly to gather and close the top of the pouch.

Figure 6.13 The finished drawstring bag.

Variation on a theme: You don't even necessarily need a casing for your drawstring. Create your bag following Steps 1 and 2; for Step 3, instead of folding down the top edge to create the casing, simply fold and stitch a ¼" hem. Poke holes at equal intervals along the top edge of your bag approximately 1" down from the top edge (making certain you have an even number of holes), and thread your drawstring through those, pulling the ends of the string tight to gather and close the top of the bag.

Figure 6.14 A drawstring bag with holes for the string instead of a top casing

Now that we have the medieval peasant's simple money pouch, let's look at creating a more elegant lady's historical drawstring purse.

Drawstring purse

For this, you will likely want to use a decorative fabric to complement your puppet's costume; you'll also need a length of matching ½" ribbon. The pattern and technique for creating this hand prop is different than the basic drawstring bags listed above, but you can use this same technique (with a plain fabric and no ornamentation) to create a more utilitarian bag for men's accessories.

Step 1: Start by cutting a circle in your purse fabric. A 10½" dinner plate is the perfect size to use as a pattern for a small puppet drawstring purse. Finish the outer edge either with a small turned hem, by serging it, or by stitching a decorative piece of lace or other trim to the edge.

Figure 6.15 The start of a drawstring purse, with lace edging

Step 2: Stitch two separate lengths of ribbon on the right side of your fabric approximately 1" down from the outer edge as shown. Make sure the edges of the ribbon are turned under and meet, but do not overlap.

Figure 6.16 Creating the ribbon drawstring casing along the edge of the purse

Figure 6.17 Close-up of the ribbon edge. This is the opening that the drawstrings will run through

Step 3: Run two pieces of matching string or cord through the ribbon casings (one through each casing)

Figure 6.18 Running the drawstrings through the casings

Step 4: Pull the drawstrings to gather and close the opening of the purse. You can add a decorative tassel at the bottom, or other ornamentation, if you wish

Figure 6.19 The finished drawstring purse

Figure 6.20 Herbert with the finished drawstring purse

By implementing different fabrics, drawstrings, and decoration, these basic patterns/techniques can be used to create a wide variety of purses and bags to suit any puppet's needs!

Broom (and Tiny Tim's crutch)

A small-scale broom is one hand prop that may actually be difficult to find ready-made. Fortunately, though, they are extremely simple to make, and can be created using a variety of materials. Either a straight, smooth wooden dowel or a gnarled stick found in the back yard can serve as the broomstick, while smaller sticks or even actual broom straws pulled from the kitchen broom can serve for the tail end. Regardless of the materials used, the technique for creating the broom is the same. Simply cut the wooden dowel or found stick to the appropriate length, and use a string to tie a bundle of the broom straws, small twigs, or dried pine needles around the bottom of the stick.

Having mentioned Tiny Tim's crutch several times throughout this chapter, it would be lacking not to mention how it could be made. In the same vein as a broom, the crutch can be made from a stick or sticks found in the backyard. You may be lucky enough to stumble across a Y-forked stick that would work very well as a crutch with little modification. Simply cut all ends of the stick to the desired length, and wrap the fork with a strip of fabric. Or, if you are unable to find the perfect single stick, you can secure two sticks together in a T-shape, wrap the T-joint with a strip of fabric, and cut the crutch to the appropriate length.

Figure 6.21 Three types of brooms

Figure 6.22 Tiny Tim's crutch, created from a forked stick and a strip of fabric

Books

As books come in a variety of sizes and shapes, it would likely not be difficult to find one (or more) that would work for your puppet. However, actual books can be heavy, even small ones, especially if your puppet is holding several of them at the same time. It may also not always be possible to find a real book in the size and color you need. You can, however, make lightweight prop books in any size and color; all it takes is a bit of cardboard or foam core for the covers and "pages" of your book, and a few scraps of fabric to bind it with. For the purposes of this illustration, a ¼" white foam core was used.

Step 1: First determine what size you'll need your book to be (the height, length, and thickness). Once you've established the basic dimensions, cut two blocks of foam core for the front and back covers, and one block for your "pages" (or more, if you wish your book to be thicker). You'll want to make the pages slightly smaller than the covers on the top, bottom, and one side by approximately ⅛".

Step 2: Next, stack your covers and pages, lining up the left edges (this side will eventually be the spine of your book) but centering the pages within the top, bottom, and right side. Cut a length of fabric that will wrap comfortably around the stack, leaving an even amount of extra fabric around all sides. Once you have cut your fabric, open the stack, remove the pages, and lay the covers on the fabric as shown. You can, if you wish, use a light coating of spray glue on the covers to help hold the fabric securely in place.

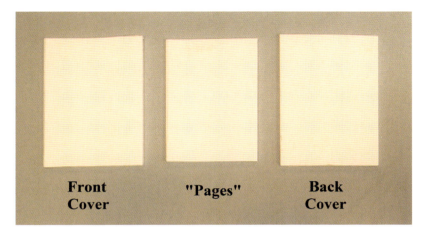

Figure 6.23 Cutting the foam core for your book covers and "pages"

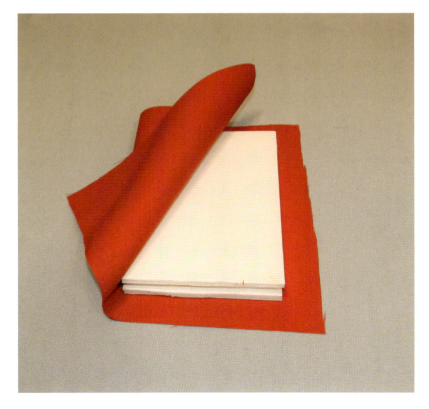

Figure 6.24 Fitting the fabric cover around the book covers and pages

Figure 6.25 Laying out the covers on the fabric.

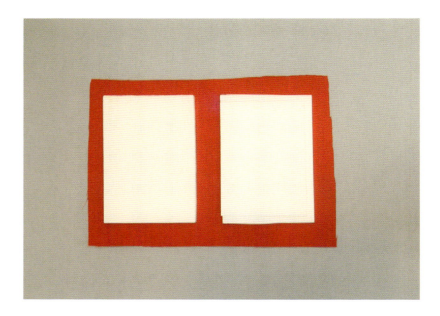

Step 3: Wrap the fabric neatly around the edges of the book covers and glue into place (folding the corners as you would when wrapping a thin gift box with wrapping paper).

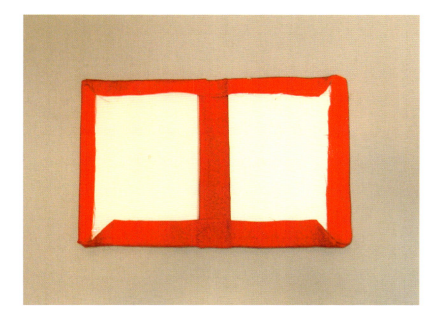

Figure 6.26 Gluing the fabric in place on the covers

Step 4: Glue the pages to the covers, again making certain to line up the left edges but leaving an ⅛" edge at the top, bottom, and right side.

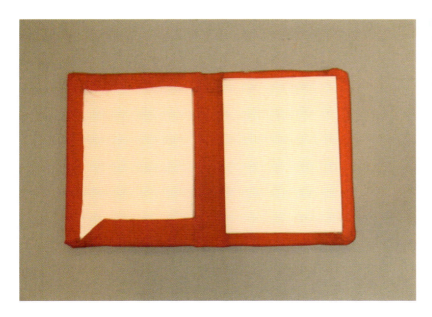

Figure 6.27 Attaching the pages to the covers. First glue the pages to the back cover, making certain to line up the left edges but leaving an ⅛" overlap at the top, bottom, and right side

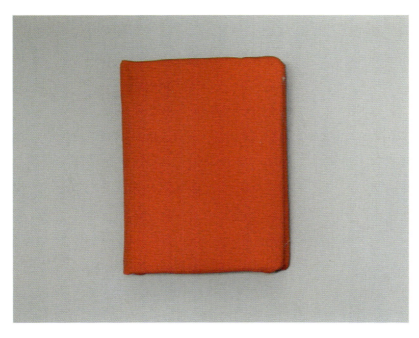

Figure 6.28 Finish the book by gluing it closed, with the front cover secured to the pages

Figure 6.29 The top of the finished book, showing the "pages" glued within the covers

You can make several of these books in a variety of sizes and colors, using different fabrics for the covers and a wider or thinner layer of foam core for the pages, for a library any literary puppet would be proud of! Or, you can stack and secure them with a scrap of leather/suede strap or belt, for a lightweight bundle of schoolbooks that a student would have no trouble carrying with them to class.

Once you have purchased, scrounged, and/or built a few smaller-scale props for your puppets, you'll find it grows easier to look at objects and materials with a different eye. You'll be able to see the potential in a variety of household and craft items, and use them not for their original purpose, but as serviceable costume and stage props to complement any puppet's attire!

Figure 6.30 A stack of smaller-scale books

Figure 6.31 With the addition of a leather carrying strap, you can create a stack of books suitable for a student on their way to school

chapter 7

Some costume ideas to help you get started

At this point, you should hopefully have an idea of how to pull together the different elements in this book to create solid, complete costumes for a variety of puppet characters. As you build more and more characters and costumes, you'll find it useful to create a photo file of historical costume pictures for reference and inspiration. Be aware that due to the size and movement constraints of your puppet, you may not be able to exactly recreate a specific costume. It's more important to suggest the line/color of historical costumes than to attempt an exact copy.

Included in this chapter are several basic character costume ideas to help you get started. With just a little alteration, these costumes can be made to fit almost any type of character you want!

Fairy-tale princess

Bodice: Using the basque bodice pattern, cut one front and two backs from an elegant brocade or velvet. For the lining, cut one front and two back pieces from a lightweight fabric such as cotton broadcloth.

Add any trim or decoration you might want to the front of the bodice. Stitch the bodice front and back pieces together at the shoulders, and do the same with the lining pieces. Following the construction procedures in Chapter 4, stitch the bodice and bodice lining together.

Sleeve: Using the larger gathered sleeve pattern, cut two sleeve pieces from a matching or complementary fabric (here Herbert's sleeves are made with gold lace over satin). If you wish, you can add an extra accent of lace or other trim along the bottom edge of the sleeve before you begin to construct the sleeve ruffle. Add a second line of gathering mid-way up the sleeve, and attach the sleeve to the bodice as instructed in Chapter 4.

Skirt with overskirt: For the underskirt, cut a piece of matching/complementary fabric, such as satin (here Herbert's skirt/overskirt are constructed of the same fabric as the sleeves), following the instructions in Chapter 4. Cut another piece the same way for the overskirt. Stitch the back seam separately for both pieces, then put the top fabric over the underskirt. Treating both pieces of fabric as one, stitch the top edges together and then fold and stitch to create an elastic casing for a gathered waistband. You can then add trim to the bottom edges if desired, and/or gather up the overskirt for a draped effect.

Hat and shoes: For the hat, construct a "princess hat" following the instructions in Chapter 5, using a fabric and trim to complement your dress. You can also construct shoes of matching fabric, if desired.

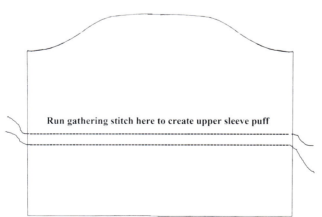

Figure 7.1 To create a double-puffed sleeve, add a second line of gathering mid-way up the sleeve's length

Figure 7.2 Creating a skirt with a draped overskirt

Figure 7.3 Herbert as a fairy-tale princess

Variation on a theme: For Rapunzel use the center-part yarn wig instructions to make extra-long hair. Twist into a single braid and add flowers and/or ribbons.

Figure 7.4 A long center-part wig with a single braid for Rapunzel

If you wish to make glass slippers for Cinderella, follow the instructions for making shoes, using clear vinyl for the upper (you'll want a stiff poster board/cardboard for the soles).

Fairy-tale prince

Shirt: Construct a shirt from lightweight satin using the "basic bodice/shirt" pattern and the larger gathered sleeve (be sure to cut one front, one back, and two sleeves—you won't need to make a lining for this particular shirt). Before assembling the shirt, cut a short slit down the center front to create an opening large enough to pull over your puppet's head. Stitch a length of lace along the cut edge, then finish constructing the shirt (for instructions on how to complete the "basic bodice/shirt" pattern, see Chapter 4, pp 53–54). Once the shirt is assembled, hand or machine-stitch another piece of lace or a ruffle around the edge of the collar.

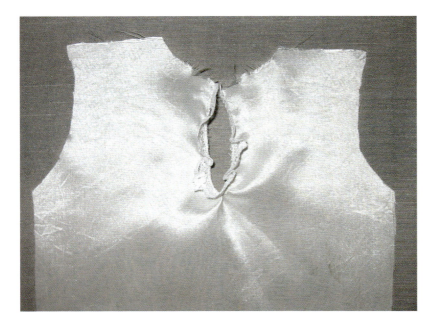

Figure 7.5 Stitching the lace onto the center front neckline of a loose-sleeved shirt

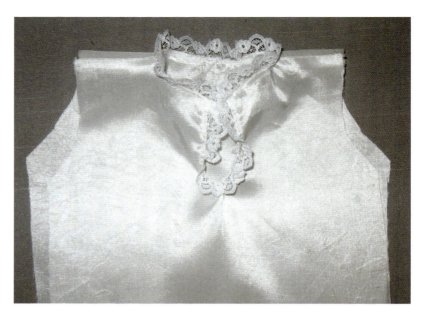

Figure 7.6 Once the lace has been stitched onto the center front, it can be stitched to the rest of the neckline to finish it

Vest/overcoat: Again using the "basic bodice/shirt" pattern, cut one back and two fronts from an elegant brocade, and one back/two fronts from lining (no sleeves). Assemble the pieces and trim as desired.

Pants and accessories: Construct a pair of pants (either "true pants" or a simple tube) in matching fabric. Add a Renaissance cap or crown. If he's truly a dashing prince, he may even have an elegant fake-fur mustache and/or beard (with a larger crown, and perhaps a grey or white mustache or beard, he becomes a king!). A royal medallion or signet ring completes his costume.

Variation on a theme: You can turn your handsome prince into a scurvy pirate. Add a few more flashy accessories, trade his crown or cap for a tricorn, and give him an eye patch. You can even add a parrot (purchased from a craft store) if you wish!

Another variation on a theme: The method for creating a ruffled shirt can also be used to create a long man's period nightshirt by simply extending the length of the shirt pattern and attaching a ribbon tie at the neckline. Add a nightcap created of the same fabric as for the shirt using the pointed hat pattern, and attach a purchased tassel to the tip. You can also construct a scraggly

7 Some costume ideas to help you get started

Figure 7.7 Herbert as a fairy-tale prince

Figure 7.8 Herbert as his favorite character, a fierce pirate. Here the prince's basic outfit is used with just a few additions and changes

7 Some costume ideas to help you get started

Figure 7.9 Herbert as Ebenezer Scrooge, complete with nightcap and candlestick

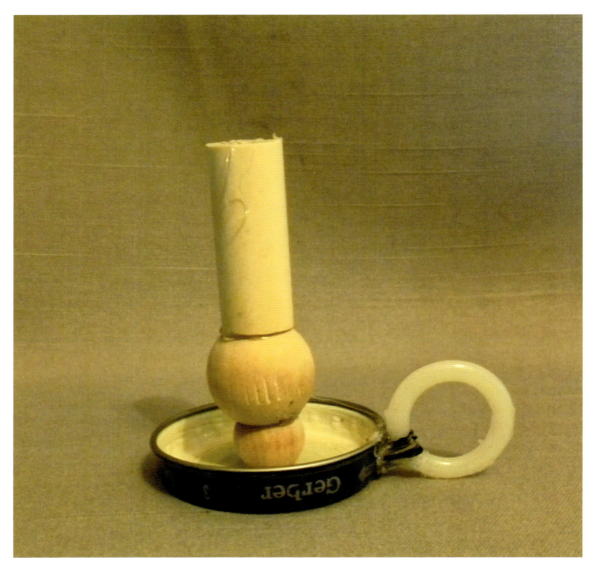

Figure 7.10 For Scrooge's candlestick, you can either purchase one ready-made (if you can find one in the appropriate size that isn't too heavy), or create one yourself from "found" items. In this case, a small jar lid, two wooden beads, a small length of plastic pipe, and a plastic ring all glued to the jar lid form the basic shape of the candlestick

short center-part wig of gray yarn for an Ebenezer Scrooge if you wish, and complete Scrooge's ensemble with the addition of a candlestick (either purchased, if you can find an appropriate size, or built as pictured here).

7 Some costume ideas to help you get started

Figure 7.11 The finished candlestick, painted with metallic gold

Witch

Using the "bodice/shirt" patterns, cut two of each piece in black fabric and stitch as in Chapter 4, leaving the bottom edge open. Create a tube skirt and run a gathering stitch along the top edge; stitch to the bottom edge of the bodice. Using the closer-fitting sleeve pattern, create two sleeves and finish the edges with a simple turned hem (you can bring them to a point if you desire!). Add a black felt witch's hat as discussed in Chapter 5. A broom can be created by cutting a wooden dowel or a found stick to the appropriate length, and using a string to tie a bundle of broom straws, small twigs, or dried pine needles around the bottom of the stick.

Wizard

Robe: Using the "robe" pattern, place the center front/back line on the fold of the fabric of your choice, and cut one front and one back (make certain to add the pattern extension piece, listed after the robe pattern, to the bottom edge of your robe before cutting your fabric). Before assembling the robe, cut a slit down the center back line to create an opening large enough to pull comfortably over your puppet's head; finish the raw edges as desired, either by serging them or turning the edges under and stitching them in place. Stitch the shoulder seams of the front and back pieces together, and finish the neck edge as desired (again, either by serging it or turning the edge under).

Cut two sleeves of the same fabric as your robe from the "elongated sleeve" pattern; finish the edges with a simple turned hem. Stitch the sleeves into the arm openings as instructed in Chapter 4, then sew the front and back side seams of the robe/sleeves together. Hem the robe as desired. You can now dress your puppet in the robe, using a piece of decorative trim tied at the waist as a belt.

Cape: To create the full, long cape pictured here, you'll want to lengthen the cape pattern as shown in Figure 7.10 to be in keeping with the size of your puppet (to fit Herbert, we needed to lengthen the pattern by approximately 11"). Cut one back piece by placing the center back seam on the fold of your fabric, and two front pieces; stitch the cape together at the side seams. Finish the bottom edge with a simple turned hem.

Figure 7.12 Herbert in witch's garb

Figure 7.13 Herbert as a wise old wizard

7 Some costume ideas to help you get started

Figure 7.14 Lengthening the printed cape pattern to create a longer cape   Figure 7.15 Back view of the cape, showing the pointed hood

Using the "pointed hood" pattern, create a hood of matching fabric and gather into the neck of the cape. Turn under the front edges of the hood and cape and stitch to finish them.

You can pin or stitch the collar of the cape closed at the neck of the puppet, and add a decorative button or piece of jewelry if you wish for a brooch.

Hat: To create the wizard's signature pointed hat, start your construction as for the Witch's hat as discussed in Chapter 5, using a fabric that matches your wizard's costume. Before attaching the brim of the hat, however, take a pinch from the inside on one side of the pointed crown to cant it sideways; secure in place with a few hand stitches. You can then attach the matching brim.

Hair and beard: To complete the look of your wizard, cut a beard from gray fur using the printed pattern. Brush the fur of the moustache away from the center on each side, and either glue or stitch into place on your puppet's

7 Some costume ideas to help you get started

Figure 7.16 Close-up of the front cape closure, pinned with a piece of jewelry

Figure 7.17 The basic pointed crown of the wizard's hat

Figure 7.18 Taking a "pinch" on one side of the wizard's hat crown to cant it sideways

Figure 7.19 Close-up of the finished hat

face. You can create hair using a strip of the same fur, secured in place around your puppet's head.

Lastly, you can, if you wish, create a staff for your wizard by using a found stick, ornamented with a large bead or marble glued at the top.

Variation on a theme: The robe and beard patterns can be used to create any number of historical/Biblical characters. Add a head covering/burnoose as described in Chapter 5 and a crook if you wish for a shepherd character.

Another variation on a theme: The same robe and beard pattern, along with a soft pointed hat, can be used to create a variety of historical Santa Claus costumes.

Figure 7.20 The robe and pointed hat patterns, modified to fit a teddy bear and used to create a historical Santa Claus costume

Red Riding Hood

Although this character can be easily created simply by throwing her trademark red cape and hood over any costume dress, Red would no doubt appreciate something a little more in keeping with her German heritage!

Blouse: Create a short-sleeved blouse from a lightweight white fabric.

Petticoat: For the petticoat, follow the instructions for making a gathered skirt with an elastic waistband. Use the same white fabric as for the blouse, and stitch ruffled lace or eyelets along the bottom edge of the petticoat.

Figure 7.21 The blouse and petticoat for Little Red Riding Hood

Jumper: Construct a simple gathered skirt with a waistband and hook/eye closure out of black fabric. Iron on flower appliques (purchased at a fabric store), following the manufacturer's instructions.

To construct the bib, create a pattern by laying a rectangle of craft paper wide enough to fit comfortably across your puppet's chest (if you wish, you can use craft paper to pattern the jumper straps as well). Once you have adjusted your pattern, use it to cut the jumper front of the same black fabric as your skirt. Place the top edge of your jumper front pattern on a fold of fabric and press flat to create a clean finished edge.

For the straps, cut two lengths of black fabric 1½" wide and the length needed to go over your puppet's shoulders from front waist to back waist. Fold and press ¼" on each side of the straps, then fold in half lengthwise and press again. Tuck the edges of the bib into the folded straps, making certain to line up the folded edges, and stitch along the edges of both straps.

Figure 7.22 Patterning the front of the jumper

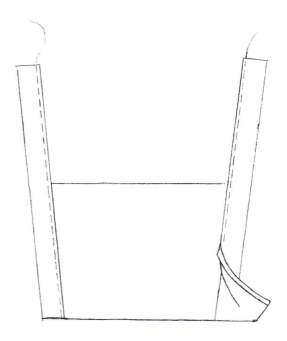

Figure 7.23 Stitching the straps to the front of the jumper

Figure 7.24 Herbert as Little Red Riding Hood

Figure 7.25 The blouse/jumper/petticoat patterns modified to fit a teddy bear, and used to create a Dorothy costume, complete with ruby slippers

Center the bib at the front of the skirt (behind the waistband) and stitch in place. Try the jumper on your puppet and cross the straps over the shoulders from front to back, to check the fit.

Attach the straps to the waistband with a few hand stitches.

Cape and Hood: Construct Red's signature cape and hood using the appropriate pattern and a red fabric of your choice. Attach two lengths of red satin ribbon at the collar of the cape to tie it in place. Give Red the hairstyle of your choice, add a small basket (purchased at a craft store), and she's ready to go to Grandmother's house! A folded piece of fabric in the basket can represent the "goodies."

Variation on a theme: You can use this same jumper pattern to create an outfit for Dorothy on her way to Oz. Construct a short-sleeved white broadcloth blouse (without the ruffles and with a back opening instead of front). Create the jumper from blue gingham, and make a center-part yarn wig two braids on each side, tied with blue ribbons. Make ruby slippers, borrow Red Riding Hood's basket, and she's off to see the Wizard!

Angel

Robe: Create a robe as for the Wizard, again using the elongated sleeves, out of an appropriately ethereal fabric. You can use a piece of decorative gold trim for a belt; in the case of the angel pictured here, however, the belt is actually part of the wing construction.

Wings: Using the printed pattern at the back of the book, cut two wings from white poster board or other stiff material (you can, if you prefer, use purchased wings from a craft/hobby store if you find them in a size appropriate to your puppet). Decorate the wings with a metallic trim; in this case, gold "pipe cleaner" craft stems were used, and glued along the front and back edges of the wings.

To attach the wings to your puppet, you can either glue/stitch them directly to the costume, or (for a more secure yet easily-changed attachment) use the following method:

Glue the center of a length of metallic trim to the top back of the wings as shown in Figure 7.27.

Figure 7.26 Herbert as an angel

Using a sharp X-acto knife or razor blade, cut two ½" slits along the inside edge of each wing where marked. Place the wings against the back of your puppet, crisscross the gold trim across its shoulders and chest, and thread the ends of the gold trim through the slits on the wings, pulling them through and back across the puppet's waist. Tie to create the belt.

Hair and halo: Create a long center-part wig following the instructions in Chapter 5, and leave it down or braid loosely if you wish. Construct a round halo from the gold "pipe cleaner" stems and secure to your puppet's hair/head with a few hand stitches.

Figure 7.27 The inside back of the wings, showing where the gold trim is glued into place and where the slits are to be cut

Figure 7.28 Close-up of the front of the costume, showing the shoulder straps and belt holding the wings in place. This technique for attaching the wings is secure, yet can be easily removed from the puppet should its costume need to be changed

Figure 7.29 Back view, showing the hair and halo

7 Some costume ideas to help you get started

All these simple costume ideas, as well as the other ideas and patterns listed in this book, can be used and altered to create a wide variety of puppet characters. You don't have to be a wiz at sewing to construct truly beautiful as well as practical puppet costumes. A few fabric scraps, some leftover trims, a pattern or two and (most importantly!) imagination are all it takes to create the well-dressed puppet!

chapter 8

The patterns

Each of the following patterns can be photocopied directly from the book, and modified to fit your particular puppet. They are printed without seam allowance; that can be added once you've made your modifications.

(Note: Where a pattern is marked "Place on Fold," fold your fabric and place that line flush with the folded edge. You won't need to add seam allowance there).

Bodice/shirt pattern

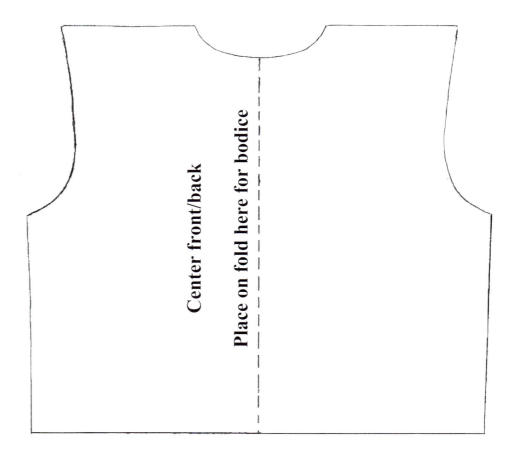

Figure 8.1 Basic bodice/shirt front. Base pattern that can be used to create a dress bodice or shirt

Bodice/shirt/vest back

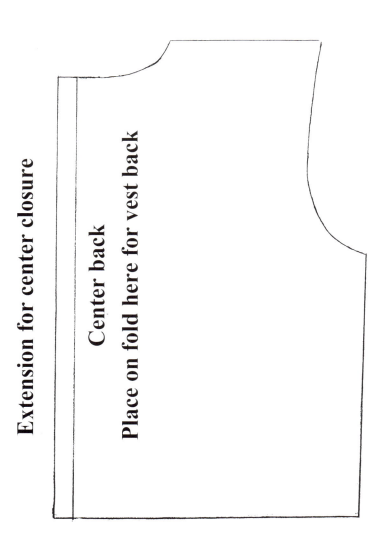

Figure 8.2 Basic bodice/shirt back. Base pattern that can be used to create the back of a dress bodice or shirt. This pattern can also be used to create the back of a vest

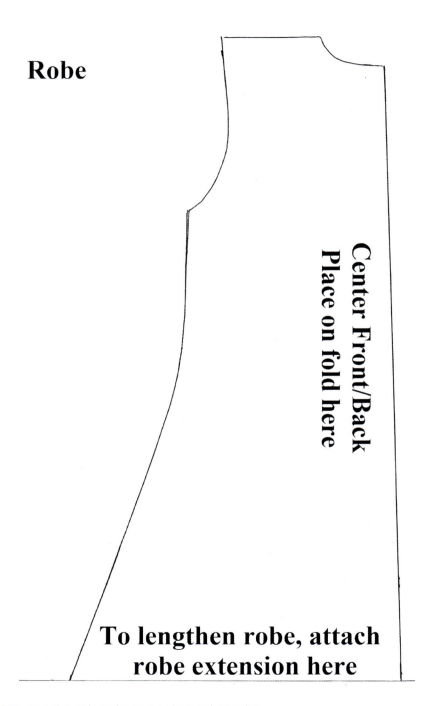

Figure 8.3 Robe. Base pattern that can be used to create a robe or single-piece dress

Robe Extension

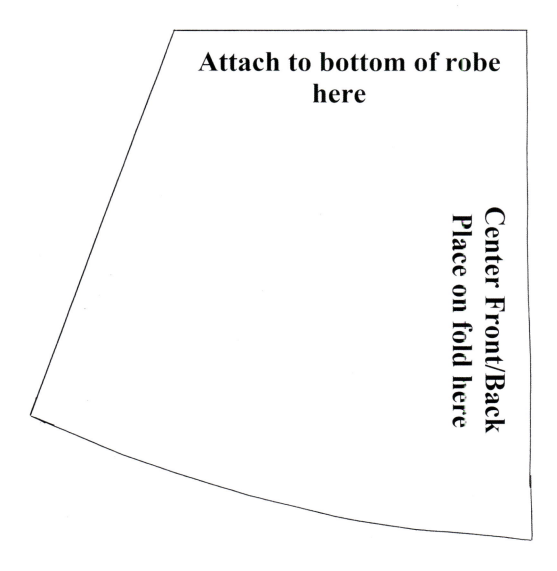

Figure 8.4 Robe extension. Pattern for extending the length of the robe

Basque Bodice Front

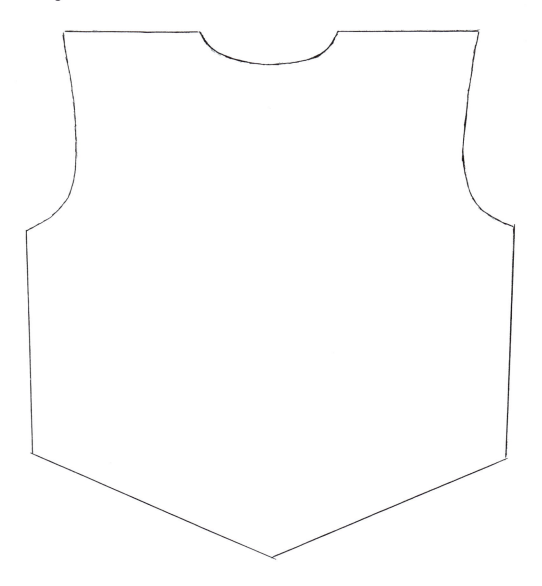

Figure 8.5 Basque bodice front. Base pattern for creating a dropped-waist bodice

Basic Sleeve

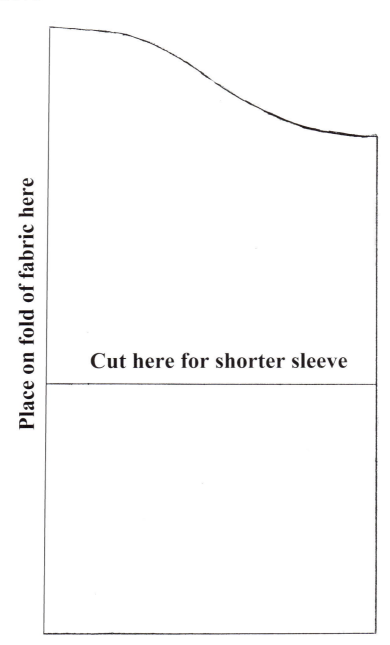

Figure 8.6 Base pattern for creating a fitted sleeve

Large Gathered Sleeve

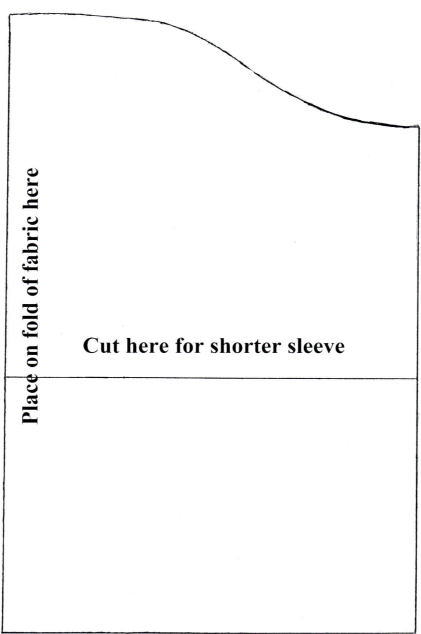

Figure 8.7 Base pattern for created gathered sleeve

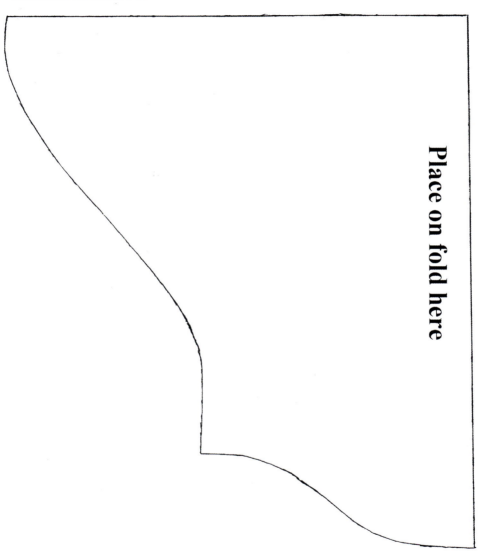

Figure 8.8 Base pattern for creating robe sleeve

Pants (these pants fit a 10.5" waist/hip)

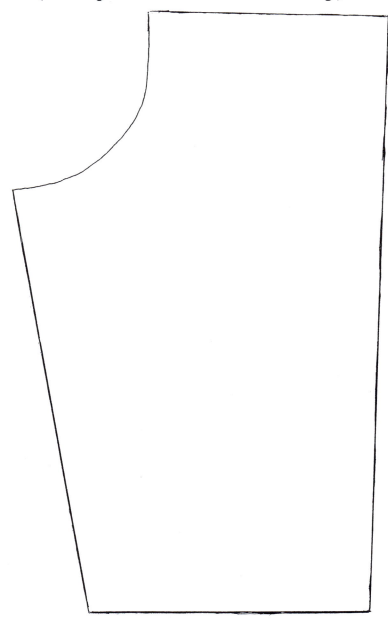

Figure 8.9 Base pattern for creating pants

8 The patterns

Tie

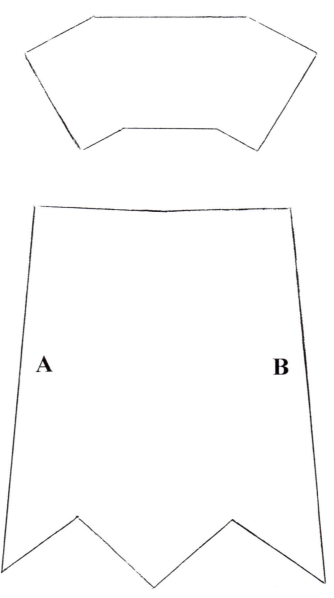

Figure 8.10 Base pattern for creating a custom tie

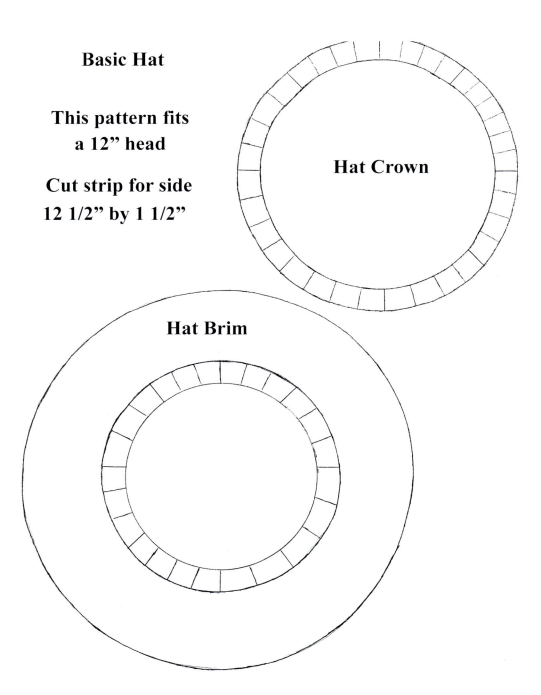

Figure 8.11 Base pattern for creating a simple hat

8 The patterns

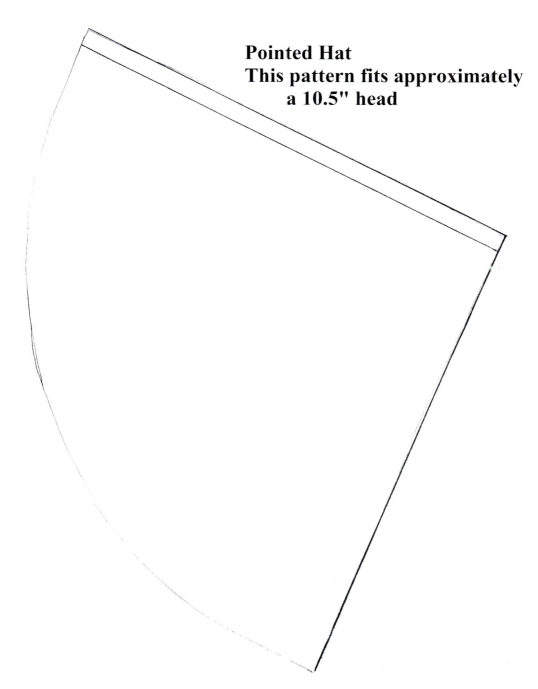

Figure 8.12 Base pattern for creating a pointed hat

Crown
Pattern base =approximately 4.5"

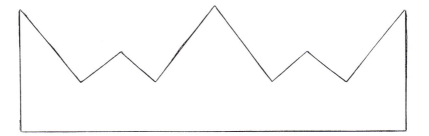

Figure 8.13 Base pattern for creating a crown. The pattern can be traced around the bottom of a plastic container or cut from poster board.

8 The patterns

Basic shoe

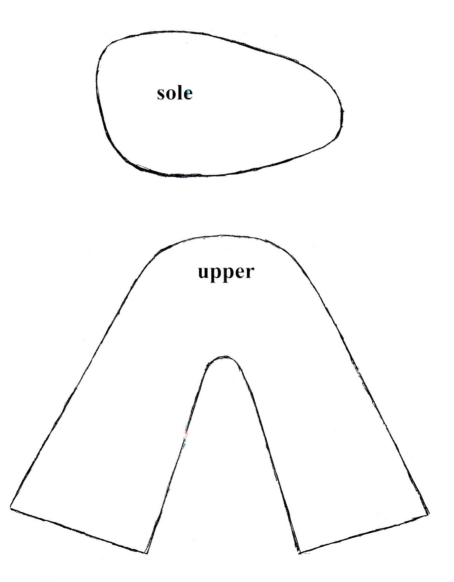

Figure 8.14 Base pattern for creating a simple shoe

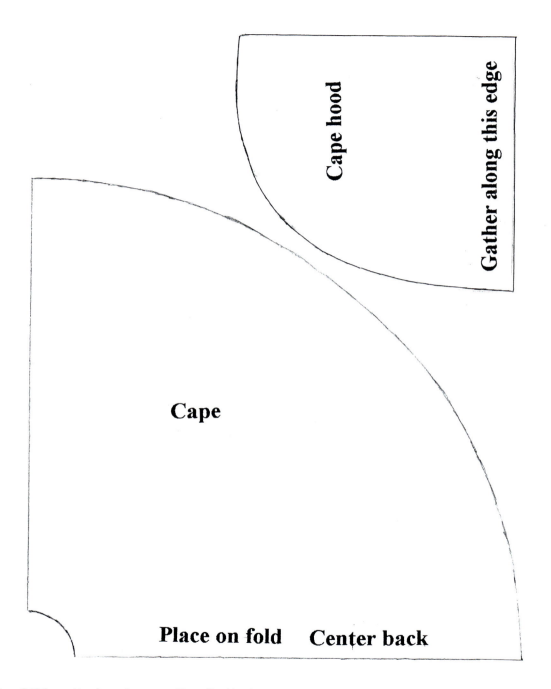

Figure 8.15 Base pattern for creating a cape with or without hood

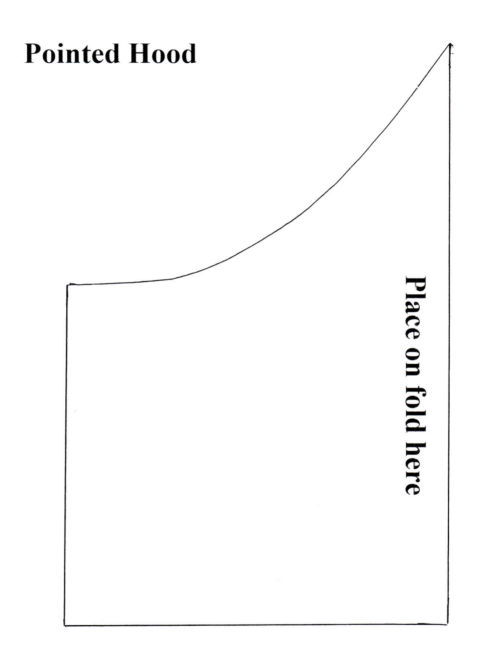

Figure 8.16 Pattern for pointed hood (for cape)

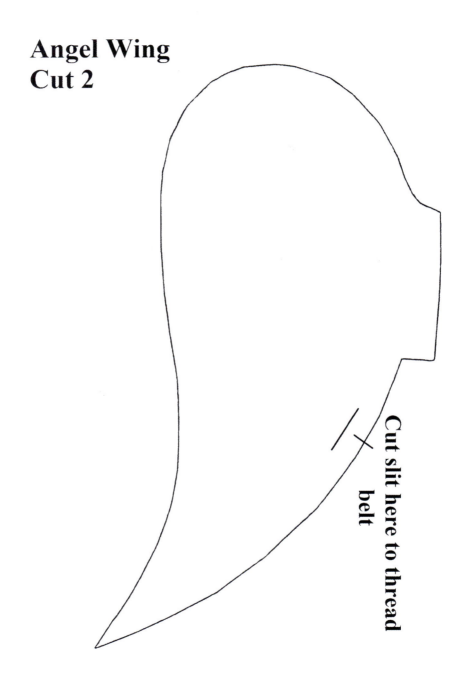

Figure 8.17 Pattern for angel wings

Beard

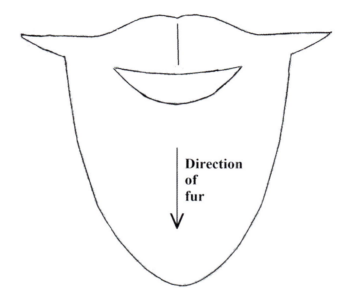

Figure 8.18 Pattern for creating a basic beard

Hand Puppet Body

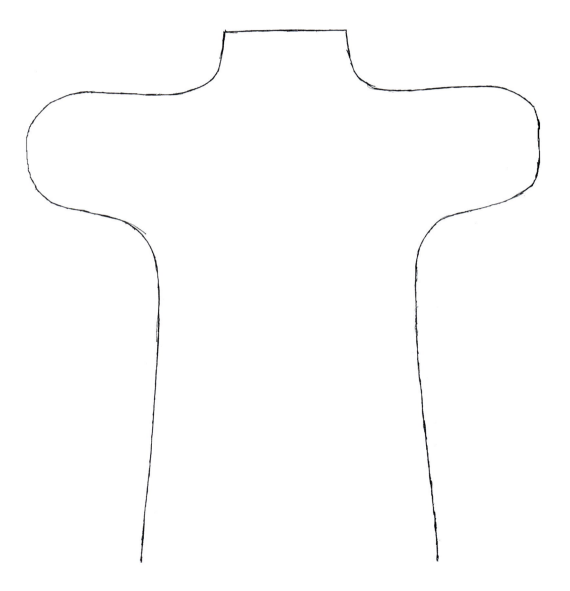

Figure 8.19 Pattern for creating a hand puppet body which will double as the puppet's costume

Resources

These days, there are a wide number of good sources available for finding small-scale patterns and ready-made costumes that would work well for your puppet, as well as appropriate accessories! The following are just a few helpful books, stores, and Internet sites, many of which were used in the production of this book:

Books

The Reader's Digest Complete Guide to Sewing (Reader's Digest Publishers, New York, 1981). A handy reference for both beginner and experienced stitchers alike, this book gives a good overview of basic sewing techniques and equipment.

Sewing with Nancy's Favorite Hints by Nancy Zieman (Krause Publications, Iola WI, 2002). Another good sewing reference.

The Foam Book: An Easy Guide to Building Polyfoam Puppets by Drew Allison and Donald Devet (Grey Seal Puppets, Inc., Charlotte NC, 1997). You have to have a puppet before you can costume it! This book is a very good guide to creating your own puppets as well as giving an overview of construction techniques and the different types of puppets that can be made.

The Muppets Make Puppets by Cheryl Henson (Workman Publishing, New York, 1994). Who better than the Muppets to discuss puppets and puppet costuming? This book teaches how to create basic puppets and their costumes from easily found items.

Best Storybook Doll Costumes by Joan Hinds and Jean Becker (Fancywork and Fashion Press, Duluth MN, 1993). A very good, small-scale patterning reference, this book comes packed with great ideas on how to create different fairy-tale character costumes.

The Perfect Book of Doll Clothes by the Vanessa-Ann Collection (Sterling Publishing Company, New York, 1992). Another great small-scale reference.

Make Doll Shoes! Workbooks 1 and 2 by Lyn Alexander (Hobby House Press, Inc., Cumberland MD, 1990). This book is a very good and easy reference on how to create period doll shoes that would work equally well for puppets.

Doll Millinery by Marie Leilani Sitton (Hobby House Press, Inc., Cumberland MD, 1989). This book may be a bit advanced for simple puppet headwear, but a good source for the proper construction techniques that go into creating period hats.

Tiny Treasures by American Girl Library (Pleasant Company Publications, Middleton WI, 1998).

A short and simple but very effective guide to creating small-scale accessories from easily found objects.

The Doll's Cobbler: A Guide to Shoemaking by Sylvia Rountree (Boynton & Associates, Inc., Clifton VA, 1983). While this book is geared mainly towards creating footwear for dollhouse-sized figures, the materials and techniques used can be easily adapted to create larger-scale shoes (and this book would come in especially handy if you are creating tiny, tiny shoes!).

Jane Asher's Costume Book by Jane Asher (Open Chain Publishing Inc., Menlo Park CA, 1991). Although this book centers on creating real-life (i.e. people-sized) costumes, it contains a wide variety of costuming ideas that can be good inspiration when trying to come up with a particular costume for your puppet.

Internet stores and sources

www.necessaryextras.com A great on-line store for doll clothing and doll-sized accessories.

www.buildabear.com The online store for the well-known teddy bear creation company that offers bear clothing and accessories that are also found at their physical stores.

www.craftfreebies.com/dollpatterns A good source for free doll costume patterns.

www.dollclothes-emilyrose/Free-Pattern-s/268.htm Another good source for free doll costume patterns.

www.allcrafts.net/dolls.htm This site offers free patterns that fit a variety of known dolls, including Barbie and American Girl.

Bibliography

Alexander, Lynn. *Make Doll Shoes! Workbook 1*. (Cumberland, MD: Hobby House Press Inc., 1990).

Alexander, Lynn. *Make Doll Shoes! Workbook 2*. (Cumberland, MD: Hobby House Press Inc., 1990).

Beau, Claire (ed.). *Hat Making for Dolls 1855–1916*. (Cumberland, MD: Hobby House Press Inc., 1991).

CC Originals. Doll Body Measurement Size Chart. Available online at http://www.cooriginals.com/images/dollbodymeasurementsizechart.html (accessed 10 February 2009).

The Fiber Gypsy. Children's Body Measurements and Garment Sizes. Available online at http://www.fibergypsy.com/common/children.shtml (accessed 1 February 2009).

Henson, Cheryl. *The Muppets Make Puppets!* (New York: Workman Publishing, 1994).

Hinds, Joan and Becker, Jean. *The Best Storybook Doll Costumes.* (Duluth, MN: Fancywork and Fashion Press, 1993).

Jones, G. P. *Easy To Make Dolls With Nineteenth-Century Costumes*. (New York: Dover Publications Inc., 1977).

Oznowicz, Francis. "Fashioning a Puppet." *Theatre Crafts* November 1986, 22: 40.

Tilroe, Robert. *Puppetry and Television*. (Ontario: Ontario Puppetry Association Publishing, 1981).

Sitton, Marie Leilani. *Doll Millinery*. (Cumberland, MD: Hobby House Press Inc., 1989).

Vanessa-Ann Collection. *The Perfect Book of Doll Clothes*. (New York: Sterling Publishing Company Inc., 1992).

Wharton, Helen B. for Bella Online. Available online at www.bellaonline.com/articles/art50945.asp (accessed 1 February 2009).

Author biography

Cheralyn Lambeth is a professional costume, prop, and puppet builder whose work includes television programs, feature films, and live theatre/attractions. After a brief stint in the Air Force Reserve, she went on to study drama and Radio/Television/Motion Pictures at the University of North Carolina-Chapel Hill. Shortly after graduation, Cheralyn relocated to New York to study at The Juilliard School to study costumes and wigs at the Julliard School, as well as performing Off-Broadway with John Leguizamo in *Mambo Mouth*. She then moved to Minneapolis to create Muppet costumes for *Sesame Street Live* (as well as a large purple bunny for the film *The Net*) and returned to New York a year later to work with Jim Henson Productions on the TV series *Dinosaurs!* and the film *The Muppet Christmas Carol*.

After her time at Henson, Cheralyn worked with Paramount Production Services, creating costumes and props for Paramount properties such as the *Star Trek Earth Tour*, *Titanic: The Movie on Tour*, and *Star Trek: The Experience* at the Las Vegas Hilton. Some of her other credits include work (both behind and in front of the camera) on *The Patriot, The New World, Evan Almighty, Leatherheads*, and *Blood Done Sign my Name*, as well as costuming work on the National Park Service film "Manassas: End of Innocence." She was also a principal character in the History Channel docudrama *Isaac's Storm*, which premiered in the fall of 2004 and can still occasionally be seen on THC. Her most recent work includes costuming work on a photo shoot for the film *The Hunger Games*, and on the Showtime television series "Homeland."

Cheralyn's other theatre books include *Haunted Theaters of the Carolinas* with Schiffer Publishing. She currently lives and freelances in Charlotte, NC, working with Grey Seal Puppets on such projects as a touring production of *Avenue Q*, along with various professional sports mascots, including Sir Purr for the Carolina Panthers.

Index

accessories 63
    fairy-tale prince 110
    glasses 69–70
    gloves 71
    hats/headwear 75–81
    jewelry 70
    shoes 73–5
    ties/neck adornments 71–2
    wigs/hairpieces 63–9
angel
    hair/halo 129–31
    robe 127
    wing pattern 150
    wings 127–9

back stitch 14
backdrop 5–6
backpack 86
baskets 86
basque bodice front pattern 138
basting stitch 14
beards 119, 121
    basic pattern 151
blouse 123
bodice 105–6
    fairy-tale princess 105–6
    pattern for back 135
    pattern for front 134
    with sleeve 53–4
books 84, 98–103
broom 85, 97
brushes 9

candlestick 114, 115
cape 62
    basic pattern 148
    Red Hiding Hood 127
    wizard 116, 118–19
character of puppet 9–10
chicken puppet 37–8
Christmas ornaments 86
clothes pins 9
cocktail pick 87
color 11, 13
Cone Puppet 34–5
costume
    characteristics of puppet 19
    hand/rod & puppets with
        practical hands 28–30
    marionettes 25–8
    partial/painted 19
    permanent vs. removable 20–1
    props/accessories 84–5 (83-85)
    puppets with legs 30–1
    shirt tricks 22
    sizing chart 24
    store-bought clothing 22–5, 46–7
crutches 83, 97–8

dart 16
decorative stitching/decoration (pants) 61
drape/draping 10, 16
drawstring bag 90
    purse 92–6
    simple pouch 90–2
dress boning 8
dress/robe pattern 55–8
    angel 127
    basic 136
    extension 137
    wizard 116

fabric paper 9
fabrics 9
    choosing 13
    color/prints 10–11, 13
    drape 10
    front/back side 10
    types 12

face of fabric 10, 16
fairy-tale prince
    pants/accessories 110
    shirt 109
    variations 110–13
    vest/overcoat 110
fairy-tale princess
    bodice 105–6
    hat/shoes 106–9
    skirt with overskirt 106
    sleeve 106
fans 87–9
Fin (fish) puppet 22
finger puppet 4–5
    with cocktail pick sword 87

gathering stitch 14
glasses 69–70
gloves 71
glues 8
golf pencils 86

hair *see* wigs/hairpieces
halo 129, 130
hand props 84
hand puppet 1–2
    basic pattern 152
    costume considerations 25–8
    with legs 30–1
    practical 3
hats/headwear 75–6, 85
    baseball cap 80
    basic pattern 144
    basic shape 76
    crown pattern 146
    fairy-tale princess 106–8
    head scarf 81
    king's crown 80–1
    mob cap 79–80
    pointed hat pattern 145
    princess hat 79
    Renaissance hat 80

wizard 119, 120, 121
wizard/clown 79
hem 16
hole punch 8
hood 127
    pointed hood pattern 149
Humpty Dumpty 21, 35–7

interfacing 9
iron 8
ironing board 8

jewelry 70
jumper 124, 127

ladies' hand fan 87–9
letter openers 86
line/silhouette 11

marionette 3
    costume considerations 25–8
markers 9
measuring tape 8
mock-up 16, 51–3
moving mouth puppet 2

needle nose pliers 8
needles 8
nightshirt 110, 113
novelty key chains 86

odd-shaped puppets (with multiple limbs)
    altering store-bought clothing 36–7
    costuming 39–46
odd-shaped puppets (without arms/legs)
    altering store-bought clothing 46–7
    costuming 33–8
    creating head/face 36
    pants/belt 36–8
    shirt 36

paints 9
pants 60–2
    basic pattern 142
    decorative stitching/decoration 61
    fairy-tale prince 110
    odd-shaped puppets 36–8
paper 8
paper board 8
paper clips 9
party favors 86
pattern creation/construction 49
    beard 151
    cape 62
    hand puppet body 152
    making a mock-up 51–3
    pants 60–2
    photocopier trick 49–51
    robe/dress 55–8
    shirt/bodice with sleeve 53–4
    skirt 58–60
    vest 54–5
patterns
    angel wing 150
    basque bodice 138
    bodice/shirt 134–5
    cape 148
    hat 144–6
    hood 149
    pants 142
    robe 136–7
    shoe 147
    sleeves 139–41
    tie 143
pencils 9
pens 9
petticoat 123
photocopier trick 49–51
pirate 110
plastic tubing 8
play board 5
props 83
    books 98–103
    broom/crutch 97–8

Index

costume 84
drawstring bag/purse 90–6
hand 84
ladies' hand fan 87–9
practical 85–7
set 83–4
set dressing 84
puppet with practical hands 28–30

Rapunzel 108
Red Riding Hood 123
   blouse 123
   cape/hood 127
   jumper 124–7
   petticoat 123
   variation 127
regular pliers 8
resources
   books 153–4
   Internet stores/sources 155
rigilene 8
robe/dress 55–8
   angel 127
   basic pattern 136
   extension pattern 137
   wizard 116
rod puppet 2
   costume considerations 25–8
ruler 8
running stitch 14

safety pins 9
Santa Claus 121, 122
Scrooge, Ebenezer 113–15
seam allowance 16–17
selvage 17
serger 6
set dressing 84
set props 83
sewing machine 6
sewing techniques/hints 13–14
   back stitch 14

dart 16
drape/draping 16
face of fabric 16
gathering stitch 14–15
hem 16
mock-up 16
seam allowance 16–17
selvage 17
straight/running stitch 14
shadow puppet 4
shirt
   fairy-tale prince 109–10
   pattern for back 135
   pattern for front 134
   with sleeve 53–4
shoes 73
   basic pattern 147
   black vinyl for Mary Janes's 74
   brown/tan felt for cowboy boots 74
   clear vinyl for glass slippers 74, 109
   creating 73–4
   gluing leather/vinyl 74
   poster board with fabric cover 75
   store-bought vs. home-made 73
skirt 58
   attaching to bodice 60
   basic with elastic waist 59
   gathered with fitted waistband 59–60
   with overskirt 106
sleeve 106
   basic pattern 139
   large gathered sleeve pattern 140
   robe sleeve pattern 141
sleeve board 8
spider puppet 39–46
stage 5
straight pins 9
straight stitch 14

thread 8
ties/neck adornment 71–2
   tie pattern 143
trims 9

vest
   constructing 54–5
   fairy-tale prince 110
   pattern for back 135

wigs/hairpieces 63–4
   actual 64–5
   angel 129, 130
   broom straw 67
   cassette tape/cheerleading pom-poms 67
   chenille, crepe, doll hair 65
   construction 67–9
   curling using steam from iron 65
   fabric 65
   fake fur 65, 66
   feathers/marabou 65
   mops 67
   pipe cleaners 67
   raffia 67
   scrub brushes 67
   stitched center-part wig 68–9
   wizard 119, 121
   yarn 65
wings 127–30
   angel wing pattern 150
wire cutters 8
witch 115, 117
wizard
   cape 116, 118–19
   hair/beard 119, 121
   hat 119
   robe 116
   variations 121–2

yardstick 8

eBooks
from Taylor & Francis
Helping you to choose the right eBooks for your Library

Add to your library's digital collection today with Taylor & Francis eBooks. We have over 45,000 eBooks in the Humanities, Social Sciences, Behavioural Sciences, Built Environment and Law, from leading imprints, including Routledge, Focal Press and Psychology Press.

Choose from a range of subject packages or create your own!

Benefits for you
- Free MARC records
- COUNTER-compliant usage statistics
- Flexible purchase and pricing options
- 70% approx of our eBooks are now DRM-free.

Benefits for your user
- Off-site, anytime access via Athens or referring URL
- Print or copy pages or chapters
- Full content search
- Bookmark, highlight and annotate text
- Access to thousands of pages of quality research at the click of a button.

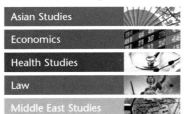

Free Trials Available

We offer free trials to qualifying academic, corporate and government customers.

eCollections
Choose from 20 different subject eCollections, including:
- Asian Studies
- Economics
- Health Studies
- Law
- Middle East Studies

eFocus
We have 16 cutting-edge interdisciplinary collections, including:
- Development Studies
- The Environment
- Islam
- Korea
- Urban Studies

For more information, pricing enquiries or to order a free trial, please contact your local sales team:

UK/Rest of World: **online.sales@tandf.co.uk**
USA/Canada/Latin America: **e-reference@taylorandfrancis.com**
East/Southeast Asia: **martin.jack@tandf.com.sg**
India: **journalsales@tandfindia.com**

www.tandfebooks.com